Theos Friends' Programme

Theos is a religion and society think tank which seeks to inform and influence public opinion about the role of faith and belief in society.

We were launched in November 2006 with the support of the Archbishop of Canterbury, Dr Rowan Williams and the Cardinal Archbishop of Westminster, Cardinal Cormac Murphy-O'Connor.

GW00481118

We provide

- high-quality research, reports and publications;
- an extensive events programme;
- news, information and analysis to media companies, parliamentarians and other opinion formers.

We can only do this with your help!

Theos Friends receive complimentary copies of all Theos publications, invitations to selected events and monthly email bulletins.

Theos Associates receive all the benefits of Friends and in addition are invited to attend an exclusive annual dinner with the Theos Director and team.

 If you would like to become a Friend or an Associate, please visit www.theosthinktank.co.uk or detach or photocopy the form below, and send it with a cheque to Theos for the relevant amount. Thank you.

Yes, I would like to help change public opinion!
I enclose a cheque payable to Theos for: ☐ **£60** (Friend) ☐ **£300** (Associate)
Other amount_____

☐ Please send me information on how to give by direct debit

Name_____

Address _____

_____

_____ Postcode _____

Email _____

Tel _____

Theos will use your personal information to keep you updated about its activities. Theos will not pass your details to any third party to be used for marketing activities. If you wish to change the way we communicate with you please phone us on 02078287777. Theos sub-contracts its data processing. Our data processing contractors are bound by the terms of this statement.

Please return this form to:
Theos | 77 Great Peter Street | London | SW1P 2EZ
S: 97711 D: 36701

Theos – clear thinking on religion and society

Theos is a Christian think tank working in the area of religion, politics and society. We aim to inform debate around questions of faith and secularism and the related subjects of values and identity. We were launched in November 2006, and our first report *'Doing God': a Future for Faith in the Public Square,* written by Nick Spencer, examined the reasons why faith will play an increasingly significant role in public life.

what Theos stands for

In our post-secular age, interest in spirituality is increasing across western culture. We believe that it is impossible to understand the modern world without an understanding of religion. We also believe that much of the debate about the role and place of religion has been unnecessarily emotive and ill-informed. We reject the notion of any possible 'neutral' perspective on these issues.

what Theos works on

Theos conducts research, publishes reports and runs debates, seminars and lectures on the intersection of religion, politics and society in the contemporary world. We also provide regular comment for print and broadcast media. Research areas include religion in relation to public services, the constitution, law, the economy, pluralism and education.

what Theos provides

In addition to our independently driven work, Theos provides research, analysis and advice to individuals and organisations across the private, public and not-for-profit sectors. The Theos team have extensive experience in quantitative, qualitative and ethnographic research and consultancy. For more information about Theos Consultancy contact the team at hello@theosthinktank.co.uk.

what Theos believes

Theos was launched with the support of the Archbishop of Canterbury and the Cardinal Archbishop of Westminster, but it is independent of any particular denomination. We are an ecumenical Christian organisation, committed to the belief that religion in general and Christianity in particular has much to offer for the common good of society as a whole. We are committed to the traditional creeds of the Christian faith and draw on social and political thought from a wide range of theological traditions. We also work with many non-Christian and non-religious individuals and organisations.

A Very Modern Ministry:

Chaplaincy in the UK

Ben Ryan

Acknowledgements

This report presents the findings of a study into chaplaincy by Theos in partnership with the Cardiff Centre for Chaplaincy Studies. Theos would like to particularly thank Rev Dr Andrew Todd for his assistance and supervision throughout the project.

The research would not have been possible without the great generosity and support of the Halley Stewart Trust, Apostleship of the Sea, the Harvest Charitable Trust and the Healthcare Chaplaincy Faith and Belief Group.

The interviews and data recorded in this report are drawn from an enormous range of chaplaincy bodies, faith and belief groups and organisations from across the UK and we are immensely grateful for the willingness of a huge number of people to give up their time to help with the research.

Finally, special thanks is due to Joanna Bryant, who over the course of a three month period heroically travelled the length and breadth of the country to carry out interviews and help shape the direction of the research.

Published by Theos in 2015
© Theos

ISBN 978-0-9574743-9-0

For further information and subscription details please contact:

Theos
Licence Department
77 Great Peter Street
London
SW1P 2EZ

T 020 7828 7777
E hello@theosthinktank.co.uk
www.theosthinktank.co.uk

contents

foreword

The biggest changes are those you don't notice. So it may be with religion in 21st century Britain.

Everyone knows about falling religious affiliation and about declining church attendance. They have become truisms, albeit truisms betrayed by sub-plots about Islam, Catholicism, Evangelicalism, and black majority churches.

Yet, while religion in Britain has been shrinking, it has also been changing, and not simply in its composition. There is good reason to believe the model of British religion is in flux. Specifically, there are signs that having long been informed by the idea that the faithful will come to us, nowadays the religious are going to the faithful – and, indeed, to the unfaithful. In short, the model is shifting from 'church' to 'chapel'.

Chaplaincy in the UK has long been associated with Christianity, and with a limited range of traditional sectors: education, the military, prisons. Even if neither association was ever entirely true, both captured the essence of chaplaincy. We knew who chaplains were, we knew what they did and we knew where to find them.

Nowadays that is no longer the case. Chaplains are everywhere, operating in every conceivable sector and from every conceivable religious base, and increasingly non-religious ones. The proverbial man in the street seems as – perhaps more – likely to meet a chaplain in his daily life today as he is to meet any other formal religious figure.

This should not surprise. In an increasingly hyper-mobile society, where identities and communities of choice are replacing those of birth and geography, it makes sense for religious groups to go to where people are, rather than wait for them to come home. This doesn't, of course, mean that the gathered congregation will disappear, or even lose any of its crucial significance. Gathering together is not simply a different way of being religious alone – it offers and provides different things.

It does, however, mean that we are witnessing a subtly but significantly changing religious landscape in which 'faith', having been associated primarily with visible – and visibly diminishing – religious locations, turns out to be rather more present that many imagined.

Ben Ryan's massive and meticulous study explores this changing phenomenon with great acuity. Drawing on desk research; a detailed, geographically-focused quantitative case study – to give some idea of the picture on the ground; and over a hundred in-depth interviews with chaplains, those whom they work with and those whom they work for, it analyses not only the spread of chaplaincy provision, but also poses serious questions about whether and how chaplains actually make a difference.

The result is a penetrating study, as comprehensive as has been so far conducted, that shines light on chaplaincy and on religion in the UK today.

Nick Spencer
Research Director, Theos

This report is an empirical study of chaplaincy in the UK which aims to plug that gap by analysing two central themes – the scope and the impact of chaplaincy.

what is a chaplain? what is chaplaincy? who is this report looking at?

why a report on chaplaincy?

As secular critics never fail to remind the world, religion in the UK is in decline, with fewer people going to religious services or calling themselves religious than ever before. Churches are struggling to find congregations, and the march of secularism is relentless and inevitable. At least that is the popular account.

There is a popular story about chaplaincy as well. Once upon a time chaplaincy in the UK was the exclusive preserve of Anglicans in a few historic institutional settings, most famously the military, prisons and hospitals, and with a presence too in Oxbridge colleges and public schools. Recently that picture has changed, with an explosion in chaplaincy roles among other religions and in new settings like shopping centres, airports and town centres. That, at least, is how chaplaincy is perceived.

In fact neither story is quite true[1] – but what is fascinating is the contradictory nature of the two narratives. On the one hand, we hear of religion in retreat, seemingly certain to play a diminishing role in public life. On the other, we hear about chaplains (primarily, though, as we shall see, not exclusively religious figures) expanding into ever more fields and cropping up in the most unexpected, unpromising places. In the course of our research we have interviewed chaplains who work in theatres, a casino, Premier League football clubs, and nightclubs.

This phenomenon, of the expansion of chaplaincy, has received relatively little empirical research, but provoked a fair amount of fascination and reaction. In particular, the National Secular Society has been vocal in its opposition to healthcare chaplains and school chaplains especially, repeatedly calling the funding of these roles into question.[2] What has been notably lacking in many of these debates has been a lack of real analysis of what we're talking about when it comes to chaplaincy and what is the actual impact of chaplains in their different settings. That situation is slowly changing with a notable rise in academic literature on chaplaincy over recent years. This is to be welcomed, but there remains a lack of accessible public research on what chaplains are, what they do and why (if at all) their roles matter.

This report is an empirical study of chaplaincy in the UK which aims to plug that gap by analysing two central themes – the scope and the impact of chaplaincy. By looking at these two themes the intention is to examine the story of chaplaincy. The report suggests two primary contentions: that today in the UK chaplains are everywhere (but what that means varies enormously between fields and roles), and that their impact, while often extremely significant (and there are some phenomenal stories to this end), needs to be considered in a broader sense than it often has been.

> *This report is an empirical study of chaplaincy in the UK which aims to plug that gap by analysing two central themes – the scope and the impact of chaplaincy.*

Part 1 looks at the question of the scope of chaplaincy, demonstrating, based primarily on quantitative research, the enormous range of chaplaincy fields, and understandings of chaplaincy in the UK today.

Part 2 picks up the question of impact and argues that if we are going to talk about impact we need a lot more clarity than much of the debate currently provides. To that end, it contains three sections around the theme of impact: what is chaplaincy for and what does that mean practically? What is the evidence we have found for chaplains' effectiveness in different settings? What are the things that enable that effectiveness?

Part 3 then looks forward and presents ideas of how chaplains and organisations in the future might evaluate, present and increase their impact, given what came out of parts 1 and 2.

This introduction began by presenting two popular stories, one about religion in general and one about chaplaincy. The fascination of chaplaincy is that it seems to be thriving in the paradoxical situation of being a faith and belief phenomenon which is growing in a public square which often seems increasingly secular.[3] The story of chaplaincy, then, is perhaps not so much bucking a trend of the modern world as representing the future for the engagement of faith and belief groups in the public square.

a clarifying note on terminology and the approach of this research

There is a serious terminological issue which is impossible to resolve in any report of this nature. Depending on the field, organisation, belief, and specificity of the role in question there is very little consensus on how to define what a chaplain is. Among the better attempts come across in our research is this from Gilliat-Ray, Ali and Pattison:

> A chaplain is an individual who provides religious and spiritual care within an organisational setting. Although this role has evolved from within the Christian churches, the term 'chaplain' is now increasingly associated with other faith traditions. Chaplains may be qualified religious professionals, or lay people, and while religious and pastoral care might be central to their role, the increasing complexity of many large public organisations has led to an expansion in the range of their activities.[4]

How far this has changed can be illustrated from the Oxford Reference Dictionary of 1986 which recorded: "A chaplain is defined as 'a clergyman attached to a private chapel, institution, regiment, ship, etc.' "

Certainly, the first definition captures a lot of the work that currently goes under the label of chaplaincy. However, it is still open to debate. Take, for example, the claim that chaplaincy takes place within an organisational setting. That would certainly be true of many chaplaincy fields, notably including branches such as the military, universities, schools, prisons, and hospitals. In those places a chaplain recognisably sits *within* an organisation. The same, however, cannot be said so easily of other fields.

Take for example, chaplaincy to the deaf, an established ministry for some decades that helps provide religious services and pastoral support to deaf believers, or agricultural chaplaincy, which works supporting farmers who might lack other pastoral or welfare resources. Neither of these sectors operates within a recognisable organisational framework. Nor, particularly, do waterway chaplains, who work on Britain's canals, or port chaplains who support seafarers. They may operate *with* organisations, but tend not themselves to sit *within* an organisation.

Even the once uncontroversial claim that chaplains provide religious and spiritual care can now be contested. There is a relatively small, but growing, movement of non-religious chaplaincy work (though their own terminology frequently denies the title – as discussed below), not least those who are co-ordinated by the British Humanist Association. Other chaplaincy fields use the title but simply do not engage very much in religious work.

Community chaplaincy, which works on the rehabitation and mentoring of ex-offenders is a prime example of a chaplaincy field where religious support can be minimal, or even non-existent.

Of course, to say that a chaplain is a figure who provides religious and spiritual care is already to broaden the field beyond Christian chaplaincy and to beg the question as to whether the terminology *can* legitimately be applied to work done by other faiths. This is a relatively recent development. As recently as 1970, there were no formally recognised Muslim chaplains in England and Wales.[5] There have been Jewish military chaplains in the UK since 1892,[6] but little other Jewish chaplaincy work until comparatively recently. Across all minority faiths the growth in chaplaincy has been a phenomenon that really only took off in the 1990s. Today, the above definition is correct insofar as there are chaplains from almost every religious background in the UK. That does not remove, however, the issue that the terminology remains very obviously Christian. As shall be discussed below in part 2, this issue goes beyond terminology in some cases to the extent that a Christian (or even Anglican) imperialism can be perceived by some to be at play in some chaplaincies. That can become problematic when those chaplaincies continue to claim to be "multi-faith".

It is perhaps with those concerns in mind that a great deal of work that would once have come under the title of 'chaplaincy' now operates under other titles, including 'spiritual' and 'pastoral care', or that titles now explicitly include 'multi-faith' or 'inter-faith' and may also include an advisory title (e.g. interfaith adviser) as a demonstration of a broadening of the field. Some individuals and even whole belief groups (notably the BHA), shun the title 'chaplaincy' completely, believing that it is too explicitly Christian and carries associations that put off potential service users.

While recognising those concerns, which will be discussed further in part 2, this report has chosen to use the terms chaplaincy and chaplain throughout, for the simple reason that the term is the most widely used and serves as the model from which these other titles and roles are drawn. It is also notable that in many fields, whatever the actual title of the role or team, the most common terms used in practice by everyone within the relevant organisation was 'chaplain' (the exception being the military, where 'padre' is universally used – albeit interchangeably with chaplain).

The other rationale for using the terminology is the fact that it is a term which, despite being under pressure in some contexts, is an increasingly popular one in others, with more and more roles entitling themselves as a 'chaplain' or part of 'chaplaincy' emerging in new contexts (as will be explored in more detail in part 1). Organisations that do not carry any of the history or tradition of the role have embraced the title and are engaging in this sort of ministry.

That in turn leads to a second note on the scope of this report. We have chosen to include anyone and any organisation that calls themselves either a chaplain or part of a chaplaincy/chaplaincy team (regardless of what the role entails in practice) or who carries a different title but is recognisably engaged in the same work as would elsewhere be called chaplaincy. For example, 'humanists'[7] work in healthcare teams that are collectively referred to as chaplaincy or would be if they were performing an identical role within another NHS Trust. Similarly, other individuals who might hold titles such as 'inter-faith adviser' or 'spiritual care co-ordinator' (among a great many others) sit within what is either colloquially referred to as chaplaincy or would be in other organisations within the same field.

This project has been conducted with a very open approach and has conducted interviews in no fewer than 20 different chaplaincy fields, accounting for over 100 qualitative interviews with a mixture of chaplains, service users and 'stakeholders' (people with some sort of organisational management or oversight position of chaplains). These have included both chaplaincies that are long established and relatively well known about, such as hospitals, prisons, the military, and schools, and lesser known (and often, though by no means always, more recently emerging) fields including town centres, airports, homelessness, sport, and the police, among others.

We have also conducted quantitative research on the scale of chaplaincy within a particular location (Luton). The intention of this aspect of the research is to provide clear empirical evidence for the scope of chaplaincy in the UK in a particular place. In a context in which real clarity over what we are talking about when it comes to chaplaincy is lacking, this provides a snapshot of what is really going on 'on the ground' in a particular place. Luton was selected not because it is necessarily typical of the UK as a whole but because it is a town with a known range of different chaplaincy ideas and expressions and would, therefore, give a sense of the disparate nature of chaplaincy in a particular place.

This research has naturally thrown up a vast amount of variety as to what a chaplain might be in different settings. It is this scope of chaplaincy that is addressed in part 1.

introduction – references

1   Historically it is possible to trace police, industrial, theatre and workplace chaplaincies among others back into the 19th century and other fields such as airport chaplaincy to at least the 1970s – so it has never quite been the case that chaplaincy was so focused on so small a set of fields.

2   See, for example, 'Chaplaincy Funding and the NHS' http://www.secularism.org.uk/nhs-chaplaincy-funding.html Accessed 13 November 2014.

3   Not, it should be admitted, in all fields and for every individual. The cuts to some healthcare chaplaincy departments are well documented, not least by Theos research in 2007. However, as an overall trend chaplaincy is, as shall be apparent from some of the material below, a vibrant and exciting ministry with the potential to change the whole debate on the future of religion in the public square.

4   Gilliat-Ray, Ali and Pattison, *Understanding Muslim Chaplaincy* (Ashgate, 2013) p. 5.

5   Ibid. p. xvii.

6   According to the Army Chaplains website: http://www.army.mod.uk/chaplains/23350.aspx Accessed 8 December 2014.

7   The term 'humanist' is a contentious one (see Spencer and Ritchie) *The Case for Christian Humanism (Theos, 2014)* but throughout this report refers to atheist or secular humanists primarily associated with the British Humanist Association (BHA).

the scope of chaplaincy in the UK

Chaplains are everywhere. Quite simply, throughout British society in 2014 the variety of people involved in chaplaincy ministry is absolutely enormous and encompasses a range of organisational settings (fields) as broad as British society itself. As an immediate illustration simply of the range of fields, the table below illustrates all the types of chaplain we have been able to find in the UK through desk research.

Broad field	Specific aspect	Notes/numbers where known
Culture	Community Art	
	Sport	Estimated at around 300 in Sports Chaplaincy UK[1]
	Theatre	
Education	School	At least 170 from the Church of England alone[2]
	Further Education	
	Higher Education	883[3] recorded in 2008, but suggested by others to be well over 1000[4]
Emergency Services	Ambulance	
	Fire and Rescue Services	
	Police	National Association of Chaplains to the Police believe to be around 650[5]
	Beachy Head (suicide prevention)	
Family and Support	Elderly Residential Homes	
	Mothers' Union	
	Mums	

Broad field	Specific aspect	Notes/numbers where known
Healthcare	Hospital (With further subdivisions into Mental health, Acute care, Paediatric etc.)	Full time thought to be around 350, but with thousands of part-time and visitor chaplains unaccounted for in that figure.[6] Others put full-time at 500 posts with as many as 3000 part time[7]
	Hospice	
	AIDS/HIV	2 projects known, each with 1 chaplain
	Primary Care (working with GPs)	
Justice	Prison	Some 1000 chaplains with potentially over 7000 chaplaincy volunteers[8]
	Community (ex-offenders)	More than 20 separate projects across the UK
	Court	
	Immigration and Removal Centres (IRCs)	
Localized/ Geographically situated	Port/Seafarer (working with seafarers within a localized port setting)	
	Waterways (working with anyone resident or working on a particular stretch of canal)	
	Town Centre	Some 50 different projects across the UK
	Street Pastors/Angels (Some studies include these as chaplains, some do not)	11,000 trained volunteers[9]
Military and related	Army, Navy and RAF	64 regular and 7 reserves in the Navy, 152 regular and 324 total in the army, 69 in the RAF[10]
	Cadets, CCF	
	Scouts, Guides etc.	
Transport	Bus	
	Train	
	Trucker	
	Taxi	

Broad field	Specific aspect	Notes/numbers where known
Vulnerability and minority groups	Deaf/Deaf Blind	
	National groups (particularly notable in the Catholic Church. There are chaplains to Polish communities, Congolese communities etc.)	
	Gypsy/Traveller	
	Homelessness	
	Irish Chaplaincy (including prison, and national group work, supporting Irish immigrants in the UK)	
Workplace	Media	
	Oil and Gas	
	Industrial	
	Canary Wharf	
	Construction	
	Retail	
Other	Bishops' Chaplains	
	Politics (including Council honorary chaplains and the Speaker's Chaplain in Westminster)	

Of course, the 'field' is only one aspect of chaplaincy. Another crucial aspect in understanding scope lies in the range of faith and belief groups involved. Again here, the scale of involvement is vast, with virtually every faith and belief group in the UK, including humanists and atheists, now having at least a few chaplains on their books.

Naturally, however, the scale of chaplaincy in these different groups varies enormously, and is notoriously difficult to map. A 2014 report on Anglican involvement in chaplaincy found that there were 1,415 reported chaplains known to the Church of England.[11] The authors found, however, that this was a vast underestimate and that the church was especially bad at keeping any records of lay and volunteer chaplains and had no records from several fields including sport and town centre. They suggest that the real figure might be anything up to ten times higher (potentially making some 14,000 chaplains from the Church of England alone). Beyond this, estimates of Muslim chaplains in the UK come to around 350.[12] Other minority faiths are likely to be considerably less widely represented given the prominence given to Muslim chaplains in several fields (Muslims are disproportionately represented among prison chaplains for example[13]).

From this we can immediately note that the range of places in which chaplains are found and the range of faith and belief groups involved is enormous. However, that fails to illustrate what these chaplains are actually doing in practice, how extensive their role really is, and to what extent many of these chaplains are operating on their own, in a team, and with which other faith and belief groups. In order to provide an illustration of how this range looks in practice on the ground, we conducted case study research into all chaplaincy provision in one specific geographical location, Luton.

It should be noted that in mapping chaplaincy in Luton this research is not intended to be viewed as something that is necessarily representative of the country at large. Nor is there any suggestion that these numbers can be translated into national figures. The intention is simply to provide an illustration of the scope of chaplaincy in one particular place in the UK as an example of the sort of range taking place in practice on the ground. Luton was selected on the basis that it represented a manageably sized area to investigate (as opposed to a large city), with a diverse population that was likely, therefore, to exhibit chaplains from minority faiths (in a way in which a rural area might not) and because desk research revealed a number of active organisations involved in chaplaincy there.

This study was designed to find evidence of the following:

1.   What fields and organisations in Luton have chaplains.

2.   How many chaplains there are both overall and in each field.

3.   What that means in terms of how many hours a week these chaplains put into their roles and how (and if) they are paid.

4.   What the religious/belief breakdown is of these chaplains.

5.   What sort of training these chaplains have.

6.   Whether there are bases or facilities for chaplains in their various organisations.

These results were drawn from a survey conducted between October and November 2014 which was filled in by a team leader or lead chaplain from each organisation on behalf of their whole team. It is missing data from a small number of organisations. In particular, the Sea Cadets were in an interregnum awaiting a new chaplain's appointment as was the diocesan chaplain to the deaf, and there were no responses from East of England Ambulance Service, the local scout group or Luton Town FC – though we know there is at least one chaplain in each of those organisations. Luton is also home to an Army Reserve base which has no chaplain of its own but does come under the Royal Army Chaplains Department – which means it is eligible to have a chaplain visit if requested. Since there is no chaplain assigned to Luton specifically, however, it is not included in these data.

Also excluded on the basis of being too far outside Luton were Yarl's Wood Immigration and Removal Centre, which is about 24 miles away and has a number of chaplains of different faiths, RAF Cranfield (roughly 20 miles away), and Defence Intelligence and Security Centre Chicksands (about 12 miles north of Luton). The Grand Union Canal comes to within a number of miles of Luton, but neither it, nor the agricultural chaplain for Bedfordshire are included since neither had any real remit in Luton itself. HMP Bedford was also too far away to be included, though it serves as the local prison for the Luton area.

These exclusions are noted both for the sake of clarity and to illustrate that despite the extraordinary breadth of chaplaincy in Luton that our survey found, if one were to expand the remit up to say, 25 miles, the hinterland contains a large number of other chaplaincy models on top of this. Chaplaincy, in other words, has a serious presence in rural and isolated areas even beyond the urban sites where it might be more expected. Despite all these exclusions, the data still paint a picture of a vibrant and extensive chaplaincy scene within Luton.

what fields and organisations in Luton have chaplains?

Our findings are drawn from **9 different chaplaincy bodies** within Luton: Keech hospice, the Luton Churches Education Trust (LCET), London Luton Airport Chaplaincy, the Community Resettlement Support Project (CRSP), Luton and Dunstable University Hospital Chaplaincy Service, Luton Casino, Bedfordshire Fire and Rescue Service, Luton Town Centre Chaplaincy and Treehouse (University of Bedfordshire, Luton Campus).

Between them **these 9 bodies covered 8 primary fields** (healthcare, school, airport, community/ex-offender, casino, rescue services, town centre and higher education) but also worked in an **additional 8 secondary fields** (court, homelessness/addiction/ vulnerable people, police, prison, retail, workplace/industrial, sport, and the council).

In total they worked collectively with more than 28 different organisations (the airport chaplaincy alone worked with more than 20, including all the companies within the airport, the police and others). In order to show the extent of this, the table below highlights in blue those fields of chaplaincy represented in our data. Highlighted in yellow are those that are known to exist in Luton but did not respond to the survey and red are those absent from Luton to the best of our knowledge.

Broad field	Specific aspect
Culture	Community Art
	Sport
	Theatre
Education	School
	Further Education
	Higher Education
Emergency Services	Ambulance
	Fire and Rescue Services
	Police
	Beachy Head (suicide prevention)
Family and Support	Elderly Residential Homes
	Mothers' Union
	Mums
Healthcare	Hospital
	Hospice
	AIDS/HIV
	Primary Care
Justice	Prison
	Community (ex-offenders)
	Court
	Immigration and Removal Centres (IRCs)
Localised/Geographically situated	Port/Seafarer
	Waterways
	Town Centre
	Street Pastors/Angels
Military and related	Army, Navy and RAF (but available on request to Army Reserve base)
	Cadets, CCF (Although a new appointment is expected)
	Scouts, Guides etc.

Broad field	Specific aspect
Transport	Bus
	Train
	Trucker
	Taxi
Vulnerability and minority groups	Deaf/Deaf Blind (appointment expected)
	National groups
	Gypsy/Traveller
	Homelessness
	Irish Chaplaincy
Workplace	Media
	Oil and Gas
	Industrial
	Canary Wharf
	Construction
	Retail
Other	Bishops' Chaplains
	Politics

how many chaplains are there, both overall and in each field?

The nine chaplaincy bodies that responded to the survey reported an astonishing total of **169 chaplains serving Luton.** This figure is broken down below:

Chaplaincy Body	Field(s)	Total number of chaplains
Keech Hospice	Healthcare, Hospice	5
Luton Churches Education Trust	Schools	12
London Luton Airport Chaplaincy	Airport, workplace, police, homelessness	13
Community Resettlement Support Project (CRSP)	Community/ex-offender, prison	59
Luton and Dunstable University Hospital Chaplaincy Service	Healthcare, hospital	47

Chaplaincy Body	Field(s)	Total number of chaplains
Luton Casino	Casino	1
Bedfordshire Fire and Rescue Service	Fire and rescue	1
Luton Town Centre Chaplaincy	Town centre, retail, workplace, court, council, sport, homelessness, street pastors	20
Treehouse (University of Bedfordshire, Luton Campus)	Higher education	11

In addition, across all these chaplaincy bodies there were an **additional 16 staff** who worked within chaplaincy teams but were not chaplains themselves (such as administrators and fundraisers).

The population of Luton in 2011 was just 203,200,[14] so 169 chaplains is a remarkably high number for a relatively small urban area (approximately 1 chaplain per 1,200 people overall). With over 50 chaplains in both the healthcare and justice fields this would seem to confirm general trends of those sectors being the largest single appointers of chaplains. Together they make up 66% of the total in Luton. That does, however, leave significant scope for other fields and it should be noted that even within those two major fields the justice section is dominated not by a prison chaplaincy but by community chaplaincy, a relatively recent and less well known chaplaincy branch than the prison chaplaincy from which it developed.

how many hours a week do these chaplains put into their roles, and how are they paid (if at all)?

The previous two sections have illustrated the fields in which Luton's chaplains operate and the total number of people involved. This section provides a more nuanced approach by breaking down what that total number actually means in practice. There is obviously a large gap between a full-time chaplain and one who can be referred to if required, but is not in the organisation much in practice.

For this purpose we defined four levels of chaplains. 'Full-time' indicates a chaplain working more than 30 hours a week. 'Part-time' is any chaplain within an organisation who works between 5 and 30 hours a week. 'Volunteer' chaplains are those who work less than 5 hours a week, but with regular hours (NB 'volunteer' is used here in that context only, and is not related to whether these chaplains are paid or not). 'Visitor' chaplains those involved on an occasional basis for particular needs, but who have no regular hours.

In total, for this question there was a total population of 150 chaplains (i.e. marginally fewer than the total reported overall since some respondents either failed to answer this question or omitted data).

Hours	Total	Percentage (of total population 150 for this question)
Full-time	14	9%
Part-time	28	19%
Volunteer	85	57%
Visitor	23	15%

It is noteworthy how few full-time chaplains there are in Luton. Seven of the 14 reported full-time chaplains work for the education charity LCET. This charity, set up in Luton in the 1990s, provides chaplains to most of the schools in Luton – which means that although they are full-time chaplains in practice they are not full-time in any single school, but rather work as part-time chaplains in several schools each. The number of chaplains actually full-time in a single organisation is, therefore, even fewer, just seven out of 150 reported in this question or a little under 5% of the total. Only one of the chaplains in healthcare is a full-time chaplain, which may come as something of a surprise given the prevailing perceptions of healthcare chaplains.

A significant proportion of the 'Volunteers' were from CRSP (community chaplaincy), but the volunteer section would still be the single largest category even without that organisation. 18 of the 23 'Visitor' chaplains were based in the healthcare or justice fields – suggesting that the policy of having such chaplains who can be called in occasionally for referrals is much more common in those fields than elsewhere.

We can also compare these data to those chaplains who receive a salary or stipend for their work:

	Paid a salary or stipend	Total number	Percentage of total for that group
Full-time	13	14	93%
Part-time	6	28	21%
Volunteer	1	85	1%
Visitor	0	23	0%
Total	**20**	**150**	**13%**

It is perhaps unsurprising that the majority of those chaplains paid a salary or stipend are also those who work full-time. The number of those being paid a salary or stipend declines significantly as we get into chaplains who work fewer hours. In fact, in total just 13% of Luton's chaplains receive a salary or stipend.

Furthermore, the way in which these salaries or stipends are funded varies significantly. Only one chaplain receives a salary that is paid for entirely by the organisation for which they worked (the university in this case, although some other organisations contributed a portion of the salary, notably the airport). Far more are paid by religious belief bodies, local churches or charitable grants.

Some chaplains are not paid a salary but do receive some financial reimbursement such as expenses or honoraria. These are listed below (excluding 'Don't knows').

	Paid honoraria or expenses	Total number	Percentage of total for that group
Full-time	3	14	21%
Part-time	13	28	46%
Volunteer	16	85	19%
Visitor	0	23	0%
Total	**32**	**150**	**21%**

Chaplains who receive no financial reimbursement at all are recorded as follows (excluding 'Don't knows'):

	Entirely unpaid	Total number	Percentage of total for that group
Full-time	0	14	0%
Part-time	12	28	43%
Volunteer	10	85	12%
Visitor	5	23	22%
Total	**29**	**150**	**19%**

It should be noted that a number of chaplains do not seem to have been reported in any of these categories, perhaps because their exact status was unknown to the lead chaplain. However, based on the data that have been reported, it is noteworthy that there are almost 50% more chaplains who are entirely unpaid (including even expenses) than there are chaplains who are paid a salary (29 compared to 20). This would seem to challenge the often prevailing narrative of chaplains as a drain on public funds and resources (or indeed faith group funds and resources) – most, quite simply, are paid either no more than expenses or are entirely unpaid (61 with expenses/honoraria or unpaid against only 20 paid a salary or stipend).

what is the religious/belief breakdown of these chaplains?

Every one of the chaplaincy bodies listed at least one Christian chaplain. No other faith appeared in more than four bodies (Islam and Judaism was in three, Hinduism in two, and there was one body with a non-religious/humanist chaplain). This seems to support the idea that Christianity continues to dominate chaplaincy teams in the UK. Of course, that makes intrinsic sense in a country which remains predominantly Christian among its religious population. Minority faiths were present in healthcare, with the hospice and hospital each having representatives of Islam and Judaism, and the hospital also having Hindu and non-religious chaplaincy provision. Muslim chaplains were also present in the justice field, as were Hindus, and at Luton airport.

The actual number of chaplains of each of these faiths seemed to be a matter of some confusion to many of the organisations. Although earlier in the survey 169 chaplains were identified, when broken down by faith (excluding 'Don't knows') the total is only 75. This suggests that record keeping and clarity over provision for different groups is something that could be significantly improved across the fields (a finding also supported by Todd et al[15]).

Of the 75 chaplains reported in this question the breakdown was as follows:

Religion	Total
Christian	65
Muslim	5
Jewish	3
Hindu	2
Non-religious/humanist	Don't know

Even with these reporting limitations, it is still striking that even in an urban space as religiously diverse as Luton in the 21st century, chaplaincy remains overwhelmingly Christian. This does raise questions about how well catered-for some minority groups really are by chaplaincy – and that point will be taken on and examined further in part 2 below.

Respondents were also asked to differentiate groups within religions. Only one of the three fields with Muslim chaplains was able to identify what branch their chaplain came from (Sunni – in that case), but interestingly all three with Jewish chaplains both knew the branch of Judaism and had appointed an Orthodox Jew.

The Christian chaplain population, by contrast, can be broken down significantly by Christian denomination:

Denomination	Number	Percentage of Christian total reported (out of 60)
Anglican	29	48%
Roman Catholic	6	10%
Methodist	3	5%
Baptist	6	10%
Pentecostal/Charismatic	11	18%
Eastern Othodox	1	2%
Salvation Army	1	2%
United Reformed Church	2	3%
Presbyterian	0	0%
Other	1	2%
Total	**60**	**100%**

All but two of the nine chaplaincy bodies to respond to the survey had at least one Anglican chaplain. Catholics were present in four of the nine as were Pentecostals (not, however, in the same four), Methodists and Baptists were each in three (though rarely overlapping), the Salvation Army in two and the URC and Eastern Orthodox were each in one field. Two fields reported that they did not know which branches some of their chaplains were from.

The Anglican chaplains were fairly evenly spread over different fields, while four of the six Catholics were in the hospital (this is perhaps unsurprising given the particular needs of Catholic patients, who account for a disproportionate number of hospital call outs and referrals[16]). The hospital exhibited, as might be expected, the largest range anyway, accounting for the only Orthodox chaplain. Pentecostals were overwhelmingly based with the Town Centre Chaplaincy, potentially supporting some expectations that town centre chaplaincy is the most Evangelical branch of chaplaincy.

It is the dominance of the Church of England which is the most striking feature. On one level, of course, it is perfectly logical – Anglicans are the largest single religious group in

England according to the Census, and as the Established Church, the Church of England has a particular and unique duty towards the public square (as opposed to Anglicans alone). On the other hand, this will also underline the suspicions of some non-Anglicans that chaplaincy is primarily an Anglican club that fails adequately to represent or support the needs of other Christian and non-Christian groups. We will return to this tension over the dominance of Anglicanism in part 2.

It is illustrative to compare the chaplaincy breakdown to that of Luton more generally:

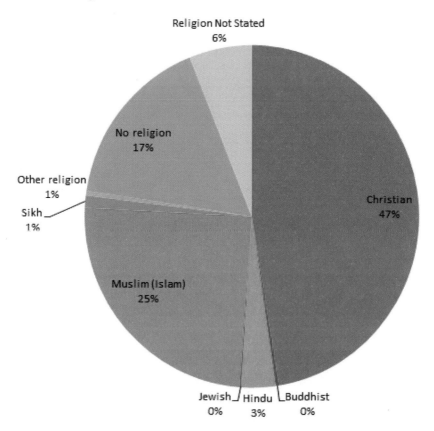

Religious breakdown of Luton (2011 Census)[17]

Notable disparities from the chaplaincy data include the fact that only 7% of chaplains were Muslim versus 25% of the population as a whole in Luton. Jews are over-represented and Christians notably over-represented (87% of chaplains versus 47% of the population).

what sort of training do these chaplains have?

A common complaint against chaplaincy is that it is, in effect, a welfare role without the appropriate training to perform as such. This, for example, has been one of the complaints of the National Secular Society levelled against school chaplaincy – if it is genuinely a pastoral support role, wouldn't a youth worker or counsellor be better qualified?[18] Our survey sought to explore the truth in that charge – are chaplains really as untrained and under-qualified as that narrative would suggest?

Three types of training were differentiated: religious training (particularly ordination), chaplaincy specific training, and other professional training. The religious training is obviously important in terms of religiously specific actions that some chaplains are expected to perform (as will be discussed further in part 2).

In all, six of the nine chaplaincy bodies had at least one religiously trained chaplain, with a further two responding "Don't know". Interestingly, the community chaplaincy programme with its 59 chaplains did not have a single religiously-trained one. This is something of a theme within community chaplaincy according to some interviews we conducted, and is a major point of departure from the related prison chaplaincy.

In total there were **39 chaplains who had religious training**, 23 of whom came from the hospital. The vast majority of the 39 were some form of Christian ordination (including Catholic deacon ordination), but there was also training via Church of England Readers, Jewish rabbinic training, and an Imam.

By contrast **110 chaplains had completed some form of chaplaincy-specific training**. Therefore, **there are almost three times as many Luton chaplains who have received chaplaincy training than have done religious training.**

This chaplaincy training included courses with Workplace Matters, Active Listening training, community chaplaincy training, the new chaplains course run by the CHCC (College of Healthcare Chaplains), Churches Higher Education training, emergency response training, trauma training, security training, the Markfield certificate in Muslim chaplaincy, drug and alcohol training, mental health expertise training, training on diversity and other faiths, and several others.

An additional **seven chaplains listed additional professional training** including counselling qualifications, a doctorate and others.

This paints a slightly surprising picture of chaplaincy training in Luton (and perhaps beyond?). It indicates that chaplaincies are taking very seriously the need to have specific training for their chaplaincy that equips them for their work. However, it also, perhaps surprisingly, suggests that this training tends to be relatively separate from religious training and especially ordination. The report on Anglican chaplaincy cited earlier, if taken at face value, would have painted the opposite story, in which Anglican chaplaincy at least was dominated by ordained priests.[19] This raises a difficult problem for religious groups involved in chaplaincy, who may be completely misjudging the resource that they have and focusing on ordained chaplains at the expense of the vast majority that are acting in their name. This finding is discussed further in part 2 when considering what it is religious groups stand to gain by being involved in chaplaincy.

> *Chaplaincies are taking very seriously the need to have specific training that equips them for their work.*

are there bases or facilities for chaplains in their various organisations?

Traditionally chaplains have tended to have access to chapels. However, the Luton survey revealed that chaplaincy today operates with very different levels of bases and facilities in different organisations. In fact, three of the nine chaplaincy bodies surveyed have no access to any base or facilities at all (the hospice, the casino and the community chaplaincy). Of those that do have a base, only the airport and schools still have a chapel or specifically Christian worship space. The airport (in addition to the chapel), hospital and university each have a dedicated multi-faith space and the hospital and fire service also have rooms made available if needed. The town centre chaplaincy has offices, but no faith space available to it. We can see from this that there must be some significant breadth in how chaplains view the importance of faith spaces and how big an impact such spaces have on different organisations. This is picked up further in the question over impact below.

conclusion

Chaplaincy is a very broad phenomenon in the UK today. The term has emerged in an ever increasing range of contexts and organisations. The survey of Luton is testament to the remarkable scale of chaplaincy, with at least 169 chaplains in that relatively small area (fewer than 30 square miles and a population around 200,000). The spread through organisations is also very visible in Luton, with chaplaincy working with more than 28 different organisations across 16 different fields.

However, this range is not limited to the diversity of their context. There is also huge variance in what the term actually means in these different settings accounting for several different faith and belief groups, and a significant range in terms of the hours a chaplain puts into his or her role and how he or she is paid.

What also emerges is that increasingly these chaplains are representing a new form of faith and belief work in the public square. Not only are they engaging in public spaces, rather than waiting in their own religious spaces, but a large range of people, a significant majority of whom are not paid a salary or stipend for their work and also tend *not* to be the traditional form of religious professional (i.e. they do not tend to be ordained).

The following part will consider in more depth what these chaplains do and why, if at all, their actions actually matter in their various organisational contexts.

part one — references

1   Reported in Bickley, *The State of Play* (Christians in Sport and Bible Society, 2014) p. 32.

2   Reported in Threlfall-Holmes and Newitt, *Being a Chaplain* (SPCK, 2011) p. xiv.

3   Clines, *Faiths in Higher Education Chaplaincy* (2008).

4   Threlfall-Holmes and Newitt p. xiv.

5   A report by Ian Gruneburg in 2013 conducted research into about 150 police chaplains – but the NACP believe the number to be much higher, citing some 650 members.

6   This estimate drawn from Swift, *Hospital Chaplaincy in the Twenty-first Century*, 2nd Edition (2014) p. 132.

7   This larger estimate drawn from Threlfall-Holmes and Newitt (2011).

8   Tipton and Todd, *The Role and Contribution of a Multi-Faith Prison Chaplaincy to the Contemporary Prison Service* (2011) estimate 7000 volunteers involved in prison chaplaincy. Todd, Slater and Dunlop, *The Church of England's Involvement in Chaplaincy* (2014) research report for the Mission and Public Affairs Council found 589 full-time employed Anglican chaplains known to NOMS.

9   Isaac and Davies, *Faith on the Streets* (London: Hodder & Stoughton, 2014).

10 General Synod paper 1776 available at https://www.churchofengland.org/media/39111/gs1776.pdf

11 One body reported having humanist chaplains but did not define how many they actually had (Todd, Slater and Dunlop 2014).

12 Gilliat-Ray, Ali, Pattison *Understanding Muslim Chaplaincy* (2013) p. xvii.

13 Todd 'Responding to Diversity: chaplaincy in a multi-faith context' in Threlfall-Holmes and Newitt (2011) p. 95 notes that 20% of prison chaplains are Muslim, compared to 12% of the prison population and around 5% of the national population.

14 2011 census data: http://www.ons.gov.uk/ons/rel/mro/news-release/census-shows-increase-in-population-in-the-east-of-england/censuseastenglandnr0712.html

15 Todd, Slater and Dunlop (2014).

16 This presumption was backed up by data from one hospital's annual report and in 'Caring for the Catholic Patient: A Guide to Catholic Chaplaincy for NHS managers and Trusts' produced in 2007 by the Catholic Truth Society.

17 Drawn from 2011 census data – see http://www.luton.gov.uk/Environment/Lists/LutonDocuments/PDF/Planning/Census/2011%20census%20data/LUTON%20BOROUGH%20PROFILE.pdf Accessed 8 December 2014.

18 A point made repeatedly by the National Secular Society including Campaigns Manager Stephen Evans Huffington Post, 2 June 2014 http://www.huffingtonpost.co.uk/stephen-evans/school-chaplains-the-chur_b_5416125.html

19 Todd, Dunlop and Slater (2014).

the impact of chaplaincy

introduction

We live in a world where increasingly everything needs to be tested and evaluated. This becomes truer still when public money is involved. As part 1 has illustrated, in point of fact, chaplains receiving significant public funds for their role are relatively rare. However, chaplains need to be able to prove that their role matters, whatever field they are in and whether or not they are paid. Organisations and faith and belief groups each make significant commitments to chaplaincy regardless of whether funding is involved. Organisations provide access, and put a lot of trust in chaplains to perform a wide range of tasks. They may provide office or worship space, training, security passes, computing equipment, etc.

Faith and belief groups, meanwhile, provide the chaplains themselves, which takes time and training away from other tasks that chaplains could have been doing on behalf of the faith and belief group. Often the cost to faith and belief groups in training and supplying chaplains is significant. In order to be justified, these commitments need evidence of impact.

This, however, raises an immediate problem in how so much of what chaplains do can possibly be assessed and tracked. Part 3 below looks at some possible ways in which this evidence might be evaluated and presented to increase impact. However, before looking at that it is important to note the key difficulty when considering the impact of chaplaincy – the lack of clarity as to what anyone means by the term "impact".

In a bid to clarify the question of impact this section looks at three themes that represent a pipeline of how we need to consider questions of impact.

- Section 1 looks at the mission and purpose of chaplaincy and how that is understood in practice. Until there is a proper appreciation of what chaplaincy is for, any question of impact risks looking at the wrong issue.

- Section 2 looks at what our research found in terms of what chaplains were actually doing that matters to other people within their setting.

- Section 3 looks at what factors enable that impact and conversely what factors inhibit it.

Each of these is based on evidence collected from around 100 qualitative interviews conducted by Theos during 2014. The interviews primarily targeted stakeholders (those with some sort of management capacity in relation to chaplains – for example a headmaster in a school, a senior manager in a workplace, an officer in the military etc.) and chaplains themselves in a bid to balance both the perspective of practitioners and the institutions in which they work. Some interviews were also carried out with service users, but these were treated as secondary to the institutional and chaplaincy view of things.

The interviews account for around 20 fields: Agriculture, AIDS/HIV, Airport, Casino, Court, Ex-Offenders/Community, Further Education, Hospitals (including children's hospitals), Mental Health, Higher Education, Homelessness, Immigration and Removal Centres, Military, Police, Port, Prisons, Secondary Education, Sport, Theatre, Town Centre, Waterways and Workplaces.

In addition interviews covered a range of faiths and belief groups including Christian (Anglican, Catholic, Pentecostal, Baptist, Methodist, Quaker, Salvation Army, Church of Scotland, Eastern Orthodox and several different Evangelical churches), Jewish (including Orthodox and Liberal chaplains), Muslim, Sikh, Pagan, Humanist, Hindu, and an interview with a spokesperson for the National Secular Society.

1. what is the mission and purpose of chaplaincy?

Chaplains, as anyone within any organisation, need a raison d'être. Unless there is clarity as to why an organisation has a chaplain the question of impact is fairly moot. Equally, it is important to note that chaplains almost always operate simultaneously within two different organisational structures. On the one hand, there is the organisation of which they are a chaplain, and on the other they remain part of their faith or belief group and usually operate with the support (financial or otherwise) of that group.

As a result, when we're talking about the mission and purpose of chaplaincy we need to consider both sides of that partnership. That is, within the context of a partnership between faith and belief groups and organisations each has has its own distinct set of aims for engaging in chaplaincy.

To reiterate, these are drawn from the evidence of qualitative interviews and are illustrative of the range of opinions we encountered among stakeholders and chaplains in different fields. They do not necessarily provide a consensus and do not necessarily tally with the opinions of all chaplains or stakeholders in any particular field.

organisational mission and purpose

1.   provision of pastoral and welfare support

An obvious and common purpose of chaplaincy from the point of view of an organisation or institution is the provision of pastoral and welfare support. How this is understood in different fields can vary enormously, however.

In some fields the mission or purpose of an organisation in appointing chaplains when it comes to pastoral support effectively amounts to filling gaps that other services don't cover. This is most typical in larger organisations which have welfare systems already in place.

> Basically there are holes in the university's welfare provision and the chaplaincy does a better job at patching them up than anyone else.
>
> (Service user, University Chaplaincy)

To this extent, chaplaincy serves as a typical "ministry of the gaps" (sports chaplain) that fills in where necessary. Often this might be perceived as a supplementary but valuable part of a broader service. An airport police officer, for example, praised the chaplains at his airport for their capacity to sit and take time to deal with the issues that would otherwise absorb a lot of police time, notably immigrants who arrive at the airport with no accommodation or employment, and whom the police simply don't have the resources or expertise to help.

In other fields, this pastoral function can be less of gap-filling exercise and more central to the whole provision of welfare in an organisation. There are fields and organisations in which very few, or any, welfare or pastoral support structures exist other than that provided by chaplaincy. A good example of this is the work done by port chaplains and organisations such as the Apostleship of the Sea, which are exceptional in seeking to help and support seafarers in a huge range of pastoral ways. Seafaring is a relentlessly tough industry and one in which the rights of workers and the support available to them are extremely limited. In such a context, the pastoral work done by chaplains is invaluable – there simply aren't other people available or willing to do it. It includes a huge amount of very practical work – such as helping with money transfers abroad, providing phone SIM cards and internet at a fair price, helping with transport around the ports, and bringing clothes and toothbrushes to seafarers stuck in hospital.

A similar story could be told for waterways chaplaincy – it's the nature of life for people who live on the canals that there is a shortage of 'normal' support structures. Something as basic as having a permanent address to which important documents (including benefits) can be sent is absent from life on the canals. Chaplains offer a rare pastoral support structure for people here.

In some of the larger fields, notably healthcare and prisons, chaplaincy operates in between those two situations. Pastoral care is a primary purpose of those chaplaincies (beyond a gap-filling exercise) but also part of a wider welfare provision. One healthcare chaplain described his role as "60% non-faith", mostly involving talking people through problems, mediating difficult situations and calming emotional patients. Another described the thing she'd found had the most impact was having a "meaningful conversation with somebody, talking about somebody who's important to them, for 10 minutes [and which] makes their day better" (Pagan NHS chaplain).

It should also be noted, albeit with caution, that chaplaincy as a provider of pastoral support is often a cheap option for organisations. This is clearly appealing to organisations keen to provide a degree of welfare support but unwilling or unable to provide significant funding for such a provision. This is especially the case where chaplaincies operate entirely voluntarily, such as within theatres. Naturally this comes with tensions – since voluntary work still requires investment somewhere along the line, whether that is in the cost of training a chaplain or simply in terms of the chaplain's time. One senior religious figure whom we interviewed estimated the cost to his group of training a volunteer chaplain is somewhere in the region of £10-15,000.

To a great extent the provision of pastoral support is the common thread of organisational mission and purpose for chaplains. There are no fields where the idea of pastoral support was entirely absent – though the range in how fundamental it is to the organisation varies significantly.

2.   response to policy

A second organisational purpose for chaplaincy is as a response to policy. There are a number of different aspects to this and they vary greatly from field to field and organisation to organisation. Essentially they all revolve around chaplaincy provision meeting a particular policy requirement for an organisation. It is not a factor at all in many chaplaincy fields, yet a very relevant, even crucial one in many others.

One common feature of this is that in many organisations chaplains are seen as an expert on religion, diversity and inclusion. This is sometimes made explicit in titles like 'faith adviser' or 'inter-faith adviser'. In an increasingly ethnically and religiously diverse country, the availability of someone who can advise on what is necessary for different religious groups in public spaces is a valuable one.

The chaplain has become the interfaith person. It's become a key role in the school in dealing with potential conflicts between students. That's how I've used him – in the difficult circumstances rather than the positive circumstances.

(Senior Manager, University)

That thought was echoed by a range of other stakeholders including the manager of a homelessness hostel, a senior police officer, and several others in different contexts. It was echoed in the NHS too, for example:

They're very good at articulating how to change and influence things like equality and diversity agenda. They have that experience.

(Director of Nursing, Mental Health Trust)

This expertise has also extended in some sectors into an explicit consultancy role. At Canary Wharf, the multi-faith chaplaincy team provides consultancy on faith issues to the businesses and organisations on the estate. One stakeholder reported that they

have taken advice from their consultancy work on the new prayer room and washroom. It is certainly good to know that that advice is there if we need it.

(Stakeholder, Canary Wharf)

This knowledge of diversity and inclusion can extend beyond religion. Explaining cultural traditions and practices is often an important part of a chaplain's role – particularly when it comes to minority groups. A mental health chaplain remembered a patient who was convinced that objects in her house were possessed by the spirit of a deceased relative. This was not so much a religious belief as an Afro-Caribbean cultural belief and they had a chaplain from an African Pentecostal church who was well-placed to help explain that belief and help the medical professionals understand what the patient was distressed about.

While unquestionably a key role of many chaplains, there should be a note of caution attached to this purpose. It can sometimes be assumed that chaplains know everything about a faith that is not their own, when that is not the case. This was a complaint of several minority faith chaplains who noted a degree of frustration that the (often Anglican, usually Christian) chaplain sometimes spoke on their behalf even without the expertise to do so. A Salvation Army chaplain also noted his concerns on the same issue:

"People often ask me for advice on different faiths and I just have to tell them 'I don't really know' – I do my best but I'm not an expert on everything!

(Chaplain, Salvation Army Lifehouse)

In schools, chaplains are often looked to to provide for other aspects of policy requirement such as the requirement for state maintained schools to perform a daily act of collective worship and to promote SMSC (Spiritual, Moral, Social, and Cultural) development.[1] These requirements are ardently opposed by the National Secular Society and other secular groups, but while they remain a legal requirement schools are obligated to find ways to fulfil them. Chaplains are an easy answer – they have the religious expertise to lead acts of collective worship and allow the schools to focus their attention on other matters.

More contentious still is the role played by chaplains in many fields in countering extremism. This has naturally been a particular theme among Muslim chaplains and in particular in prisons and education. The logic to this, on one level, seems plausible enough: if a responsible Islamic religious figure is in place to lead worship and teach people a form of religion that doesn't lead them down an extreme route then that is of clear benefit to an organisation and to society more widely. A number of Muslim chaplains in prisons (and other fields) are now funded in large part with that purpose expressly in mind.[2]

3.   creating community and ethos

A third organisational purpose of chaplaincy might broadly be summarised as creating community and ethos. An important element in several sectors, but most obviously the military, is the ceremonial and traditional chaplaincy function. The role they play in funerals, repatriations and throughout military life is central to the sense of camaraderie and community. As an RAF chaplain reported, "chaplaincy is woven into the life of the institution. Commanders don't want to go to war without a chaplain."

That was echoed by a former senior army officer who noted the importance of the chaplain in providing the "moral component of the military" and "the will to fight as a force for good". He too noted that commanders view chaplains as an essential part of planning for an operation.

Ceremonies, particularly collective acts of remembrance, provided some of the most striking stories from chaplains in a range of very different contexts. A chaplain to a hospice that specialised particularly in AIDS/HIV noted the importance of having someone able to take funerals in a small and close community. A workplace chaplain shared the following story:

> I had a phone call from a senior manager saying that one of his employees had collapsed in an open plan office and died on his way to hospital. So we talked about how we could support people. The guy who died was a Muslim, but his wife was a Catholic. [The] issue with that was the funeral was in a mosque and there was a burial. A lot of colleagues wanted to go but didn't want to go to the mosque for various reasons. So my Muslim colleague and I went along and explained to people what to expect in a mosque. For those who felt they couldn't go we had

a room and there were teas and coffees and they could talk and do what they needed. They still talk about that.

(Lead chaplain, workplace chaplaincy)

Perhaps even more striking was the story shared by staff and chaplains from the Apollo Theatre in London's West End, which made the news after a dramatic roof collapse in 2013. They asked the chaplain and a colleague to do a blessing of the reopened theatre. She reports:

> The two ministers who did it were brilliant – we didn't know what they'd do before hand, but it was incredibly moving. [The chaplain] communicated wonderfully the trauma in exactly the right way. They had the ability to give comfort and lead renewal… Then we had a procession around the theatre, included everyone in active participation. Everyone joined the procession and made peace with the place. People were stunned.

(Theatre owner)

Ceremonies and traditions can have a phenomenal impact on creating a sense of community and appreciating the values and ethos of an organisation and chaplains in many fields play a huge part in that. Even something like a carol service for Christmas can have an enormous impact on people. A number of interviewees from the Metropolitan Police when asked what their best memory of the chaplain or chaplaincy service was immediately responded that the annual carol service really mattered to them.

The creation of community can have other, less formalised aspects. Many chaplains spoke of the importance in their work of building relationships and befriending people. Those links and ties are an important part of connecting and building up many different fields. A number of chaplains in very different fields spoke about the importance of simply sitting in a canteen or walking round saying "hi" to everyone. This was echoed by a number of stakeholders who spoke about how that little relationship was important in creating a good atmosphere around the place. It also created in a number of cases a sense of availability that was seen as very important. A senior manager at an airport summed up a number of stakeholder interviews when he reported,

> the last chaplain used to say to me 'if things are getting on top of you, let me know.' I haven't had to use them but it's good to know if I need to speak to someone, and I know they're there.

4. mediation and calming role

Whereas the previous three aspects are often discussed in chaplaincy, this one was less anticipated before the research was conducted. Nevertheless, it proved to be an essential part of why institutions supported their chaplaincies in a range of contexts. In prisons and Immigration and Removal Centres (IRCs) chaplains were reported to be a rare broker during riots or difficult periods. One IRC chaplain told a story about a riot that had been going on for some time, and had involved almost all the buildings and facilities being damaged – except the faith rooms. The ringleaders had barricaded themselves in a particular room and were refusing to negotiate with staff. At that point the chaplain had turned up in his dog collar, was invited in, and had successfully calmed the situation within only a few hours.

These are extreme scenarios, but they are replicated on a more modest scale in other contexts too. A senior university member of staff reported on the importance of the chaplain in calming down severe tensions between groups on campus.

> In 2008/2009, there were lots of Israel-Palestine problems on campus, and Muslim students who felt targeted by the press, and assumed to be extremists.
>
> (University Manager)

Having a calm mediator between the groups was something that the university valued immensely. There were other stories of chaplains acting as that trusted figure who could calm people down and serve as a broker between schools and parents, calming irate and confused families in courts and airports and even, in the case of Luton Town Centre Chaplaincy, between the English Defence League and the police. It was also a frequently cited important feature of healthcare chaplaincy, with chaplains persuading patients to take medication, or families to allow hospital treatment and mediating between healthcare practitioners and religious patients (for example on issues like blood transfusions or diet).

A related role is the work of community chaplains (chaplains to ex-offenders) who provide mentoring to ex-offenders as they attempt to re-habilitate themselves into society. The chaplain provides a point of continuity and support and can serve as a mediator between the ex-offender and churches and social services.

5.   critical feedback

In several fields we encountered chaplains who were appointed in part to provide a critical voice within organisations. Christian chaplains in particular like to use the Old Testament imagery of being a prophet – holding a mirror up to the organisation. Such a role was explicitly noted by stakeholders in a number of fields – notably among charities that work with homelessness and vulnerable people (several of which explicitly employed the chaplain in part to provide that role).

The chaplains to Canary Wharf are beginning a process of looking at ethics in finance, and several sport chaplains spoke in strong terms of a role as the conscience of a club. One had been involved in challenging the club's decision to choose a controversial shirt sponsor;

another had worked immensely hard when a club had gone into administration to fight for low paid staff that had not been paid. This may seem like a role which shouldn't appeal to an organisation – tantamount to trouble making. Yet stakeholders time and again subverted that expectation and praised the chaplain for being able to speak up and keep an organisation honest. An NHS manager, for example, reported that:

> sometimes you need someone who isn't too much in the system to tell it like it is and tell everyone what we're doing isn't the way to do things. It isn't always popular at the time but you look back and you see why they did it.
>
> (NHS Trust manager)

Of course, there are cases when some organisational purposes are in tension with others – which can reduce the chaplaincy role or make it more challenging. For example, where a chaplaincy has a base that takes up space in an airport or shopping centre that is in clear tension with an organisational imperative to make money from renting out retail space.

faith and belief group mission and purposes

The mission and purpose of faith and belief groups can basically be divided into inward facing purposes (things for the direct benefit of adherents to the group) and outward facing purposes (things that benefit the group as whole but are aimed at those outside the group).

Again, these themes are based on findings from qualitative interviews. In this case particular focus has been placed on chaplains and religious stakeholders (including, for example, senior figures from different Christian churches and other faith groups) in order to get as full a perspective as possible on how religious and belief groups view their involvement in chaplaincy.

1.   inward facing mission and purposes

It is not surprising that a common purpose of a religion and belief group's engagement in chaplaincy is to provide, at least in part, for adherents of their own group. The scope of this is very broad – it can include everything from leading Muslim prayers on Fridays, providing Christian sacraments such as the Eucharist to offering services like anointing the sick, performing weddings and baptisms, and conducting funerals. The importance of these services to some service users cannot be overstated. A chaplain for the Apostleship of the Sea spoke movingly of the extraordinary hunger of many Filipino sailors to receive the Eucharist when possible – with seafarers on duty putting their heads through the windows to receive communion. Funerals matter immensely in a wide range of settings – but especially those where death is a constant part of the setting – such as hospices, hospitals, the military, and emergency services.

Chaplains, as we shall see below, often have a particular appeal to people of their own faith, even if what they are doing is nothing more than talking to someone or sitting with them. A Catholic healthcare chaplain was called to a hospital because a patient (who was not registered as a Catholic) was desperate to see a Catholic priest before his operation. The patient was hysterical and convinced that they were not going to survive the operation and wanted to be received into the Church before they died. The chaplain sat down with the patient, calmed him down and told him he needed to have his operation, but that the chaplain would be waiting for him afterwards and that later he would invite all the nurses and the patient's family and they could do the baptism then. This reassured the patient who then went to have his operation, and helped the doctors and nurses, who had been struggling to engage with the patient, but it needed a Catholic priest to do it – the patient wasn't interested in talking to anyone else, religious or otherwise.

This role also might include advocacy for the needs of particular adherents. This has been seen particularly in regard to minority faiths lobbying for more awareness of their needs in different contexts – whether that is the provision of Kosher and Halal food, an appreciation of the difficulties surrounding fasting, different religious festivals or different ways of dress, chaplains have often had a role in very different contexts in advocating ways of living together that allow for diversity and inclusion. Examples include Further Education chaplains involved in planning with the institution how to manage exams around Ramadan and workplace chaplains planning with companies how to provide an appropriate faith space for Muslim prayers.

A final interesting aspect is the role that chaplains can play in challenging and changing the culture within a religion and belief group. Chaplains operate in that strange counter-cultural position as faith figures in the public square. There is always a danger in that situation of groups retreating from the public square and becoming very insular, struggling to engage with 'real-world' issues. Chaplaincy offers a useful antidote to some of these tendencies.

The role of Muslim chaplains in this context has been considered in particular in the literature.[3] This was also backed up in our findings. Chaplaincy represents a relatively cutting edge approach to religious provision of services. Muslim chaplaincy has been breaking new ground in building up Muslim inter-faith work and in providing new expressions of Muslim leadership (not least for women). A Jewish chaplain discussing his interactions with a Muslim chaplain colleague said how unusual and refreshing it was to move beyond "dialogue" to "actually working together towards the same role".

This is not unique to Islam. A Town Centre chaplain, noting the relatively Evangelical make-up of Town Centre chaplains compared to other fields, speculated that that might be because of traditional Evangelical reticence over inter-faith work. He suspected that chaplaincy was changing the picture on that as Evangelicals increasingly worked in chaplaincy alongside other groups. The Apostleship of the Sea, a Catholic chaplaincy charity to seafarers, has appointed an increasingly large proportion of lay chaplains (including female lay chaplains) to ports across the UK. At a time when there is a well-publicised chronic shortage of priests in the Catholic Church, this represents a pioneer ministry that might ultimately have a wider impact.

This impact is also present in the way in which some chaplains have taken on a role empowering and developing the leadership of people of their faith group in their fields. A good example of this was the work done by the Muslim chaplain at Canary Wharf, who has been working with the different Muslim groups in the companies there to develop leaders for Friday prayers. Unusually for a Muslim chaplain, he does not tend to lead these prayers himself, but prefers to help others to do it for themselves. Similarly, chaplains in education were often running schemes to help people better understand their faith and take on new responsibilities. At Winchester University, most strikingly, the chaplaincy is now involved in a major project that will engage all students, across the different subjects and departments, in exploring big questions including faith and spirituality.

2. outward facing mission and purposes

Picking up once again the two stories with which the introduction started – of a decline in religion but a growth in chaplaincy, it is worth noting that chaplaincy increasingly now represents the face of faith and belief in this country. Fewer and fewer people go to churches or religious services, so if faith and belief groups want to have a presence in the public square they need to go out and prove their value.

As part of being the public face of faith and belief, chaplains have a wonderful opportunity to educate and change perceptions of what it is to be a member of a particular group. A Sikh healthcare chaplain summed this up, saying, "People see my turban and they think I'm the Taliban! Now I get the chance to tell them who I am, what it all means."

For minority faiths in particular, the chaplain often represents the only person of that faith that other staff regularly come into contact with. He or she has a powerful ability to inform and change perceptions as a result. What might seem like a strange or alien tradition or unreasonable request can be explained and tensions eased as a result.

Perceptions can also be changed simply by virtue of the chaplain's existence, for example, the presence of an AIDS chaplain where the reputation of the Church for empathy and care is (not without reason) subject to severe criticism. Simply by virtue of, in this case, the Church of Scotland's willingness to engage in such areas, chaplains can change narratives about what faith groups do or say. A vast number of interviewees talked about how people had changed their mind about chaplains and even religion more generally. One service user, talking about higher education chaplains said, "I would expect every vicar to be sexist, racist and homophobic. Haven't found this is true in this particular case."

A theatre chaplain had been experiencing significant hostility from a member of staff who slowly came round to them, to the extent that they now introduce the chaplain to other members of staff as "the vicar who's going to take my funeral".

> A Sikh healthcare chaplain summed this up, saying, "People see my turban and they think I'm the Taliban! Now I get the chance to tell them who I am, what it all means".

It would be dishonest not to concede to secular critics that this aspect of the role can be seen in terms of evangelism. A National Secular Society spokesman was particularly nervous about chaplaincy in schools seeing evangelism as a priority over pastoral support.

From our research we found enormous discrepancies in how chaplains in different fields viewed evangelism. In most sectors there was a real reticence and a concern not to be 'proselytising' while being open to talk to people who requested it about faith issues. In some fields this was effectively a non-issue. Catholic chaplains to ports, for example, encounter so many Filipino and East European seafarers that the context is overwhelmingly Catholic anyway. In others, notably in healthcare and some workplace chaplaincies, there was a clear sense in which proselytism was an absolute 'no go area'.

However, in others there was a more open sense that evangelism was a legitimate activity for a chaplain to be working on, albeit rarely if ever in an aggressive or unsolicited way. For example, while one sport chaplain, when asked what he saw as the purpose of his role, immediately answered "it must first and foremost to be to win souls for the kingdom of God", he was careful to define that that role could never be forced on anyone. In common with several other sport chaplains he quoted the Sports Chaplaincy UK maxim that chaplains should be "pastorally proactive and spiritually reactive" – i.e. a conversations about God was only appropriate if the service user brought it up. In general, sport chaplains and town centre chaplains were more open that other fields to talking about evangelism, probably not least because those fields were the ones which proportionally seemed to feature the most Evangelical Christian chaplains (as part 1 indicates in Luton). One university chaplain was also notably happy to talk about their role in terms of "pre-evangelism" or even "pre-pre-evangelism" – as a process of warming people up to be more open to the idea that they might become religious in the future.

This also raises a question for faith and belief groups generally about the purpose of such activity. If the hope is to convert people to a particular faith or denomination then clearly there is a benefit to the religious group in question investing in chaplaincy. In practice, however, very few if any chaplains that we came across talked in any such language. At most, the intention seemed on the whole to be to encourage and deepen faith of any description. An interesting aspect of this was raised by a sports chaplain who was trying to persuade local churches to invest in chaplaincy despite the fact that, since games were on a Sunday, there was no chance of those sportsmen ever coming to those churches – at best he was "planting some seeds".

We should also not ignore, however, the extent to which much of this chaplaincy provision is given up by faith and belief groups with very little anticipation of receiving anything in return. This is often a doctrinally-based phenomenon – whether it is the Christian vocation to the poor and sick, the concept of *Sewa* or *Seva* (selfless service) in many Indian religions including Sikhism and Hinduism, or *Khidmah* in Islam, there is a common thread through many religious chaplaincies of service for its own sake.

shared mission and purposes

Aside from those missions and purposes that belong primarily to either an organisation or to a faith and belief group, there are some areas of such overlap that they merit inclusion in a shared section.

One essential aspect of this is the link a chaplain can provide between an organisation and community groups. Some Christian charities used their chaplains in part to form links with local churches in order to raise funds and advertise services. Police chaplains were sometimes employed with the intention of creating a link between the police and faith groups. A senior police officer talked about his chaplain as providing

> inroads to faith communities… we are invited to places of worship like the mosque. They give you access to an entire community of people and [are] good for police reputation – serve as ambassadors to communities.
>
> (Senior Police Officer)

Further and Higher Education establishments had both found chaplains a good way of supporting community interaction, with one FE college putting on a major Sikh feast on campus. One of the most striking stories though came from the Scottish AIDS chaplain who had pioneering work in talking to African pastors and faith leaders to enlist their help in getting people tested for HIV, Hepatitis C and other diseases, since it had been found that people were more likely to get a check if they were encouraged to do so by their pastor.

Secondly, there is a point of shared mission and purpose in the very simple fact that organisations are increasingly expected to provide provision for religion, spirituality and pastoral care. This demand side of the debate was well summarised by the atheist financial director of a UK university who, when discussing funding decisions for the chaplaincy was swung eventually by the simple reality that it came down to a basic "supply and demand argument – it's important to lots of individual people of faith, regardless of what I might personally think". He and his colleagues also noted independently the appeal of being able to point to world-class faith facilities at a time when the university market for students is very competitive. Anything that marks a university out above its competitors is a marketable asset.

conclusion

The simple question "what are chaplains for" is all too rarely asked in analyses of impact. The range in how that question might be answered, as shown above, is significant when it comes to trying to measure impact. Without real clarity on what a chaplain is for in a particular organisation it is impossible even to think through how impact ought to be measured.

the evidence of impact

The previous section highlighted the tension over how the impact of chaplaincy is to be assessed. Unless there is a full appreciation of both what chaplains are and the whole breadth of their remit, an impact assessment is likely to miss some of what makes chaplains important in their particular context. This section moves beyond that claim to examine some of the ways in which that mission and purpose has been realised in practice – i.e. what is the evidence of chaplains executing that mission and purpose well?

While the following section focuses on ways of presenting and improving impact in the future, this one looks instead at a mixture of different pieces of evidence drawn from different sources. It draws on some limited data sources presented by chaplains and organisations during our research – including records of visits and referrals from different fields. It also draws on evidence drawn from the qualitative interviews we conducted over 2014. These interviews offered both direct evidence of the impact of chaplains (e.g. explicit notes on what a chaplain has done to create change) and also indirect evidence (e.g. an implication of change based on an inference from an interview). They are drawn from a mixture of chaplains, service users and stakeholders (those with some sort of oversight or management capacity over chaplains within an organisation).

This section looks at the evidence in four main areas that closely overlap with the various mission and purposes sections laid out above in the previous part.

- **First, evidence of where a chaplain or chaplaincy has caused a change in organisational practice**. This relates to examples of chaplains actively causing a change in the way in which an organisation does something.

- **Second, evidence of a change in atmosphere or sense of community.** This relates to efforts made in the mission to improve cohesion and in a mediating/calming role. This evidence is particularly taken from stakeholders.

- **Third, the impact on service users** (mostly concerned with the pastoral and welfare work). This includes the direct testimony of service users as well as indirect evidence from stakeholders and chaplains themselves.

- **Finally, the evidence of increased organisational support or buy-in.** This concerns evidence of how organisations have responded to their chaplains in a positive way as a result of chaplaincy successes. Again, stakeholders are particularly important in evaluating this.

evidence of change in organisational practice

One area in which we found chaplains who had a significant impact on organisational practice was in mental health. Healthcare chaplaincy has been the most contested and pressurised field of chaplaincy in recent years, with Worcestershire Acute Hospitals Health Trust hitting the headlines in 2006 after threatening to cut almost all chaplaincy staff.[4] However, perhaps because of that increased pressure and scrutiny, and the financial cuts that have only become tougher since the austerity policies of the Coalition Government, some healthcare chaplaincies have been extremely innovative and noteworthy in what they now do.

In the mental health hospital that we visited, the director of spiritual care had an important role within the hospital in changing policies in response to when things went wrong. For example, after the death of a particular patient the nurses had felt it would be traumatic to leave the patient as they had been, and cleared everything away, including the body. However, the patient had been a Sikh and the family were extremely upset that the body had been moved before they arrived. The situation escalated quickly, with the hospital staff not understanding why. Subsequently hospital policy, with the input of the chaplains, has been changed to reflect the religious sensitivities and practices of Sikh patients, in order to avoid that difficult situation arising again.

The chaplains in this context were responsible for educating staff and changing policies to reflect the sensitivities of patients' religious beliefs. In another case, a doctor had assumed that because of the particular faith background of a patient they would inherently not be at risk of suicide – again the chaplains were involved in educating against such assumptions and working on policies and with staff training.

In other cases the change in organisational practice was more to do with the actual clinical work. The chaplains were called on to give their expertise on whether what a patient believed or did was within the bounds of normal behaviour for a particular belief structure or whether it was part of their condition. One chaplain gave an example of Afro-Caribbean religious traditions that involved a lot of speaking in tongues, which had led to doctors and nurses sedating patients or treating that as a symptom of their condition – not realising that within that cultural and religious tradition that behaviour was quite normal, and not *necessarily* part of their condition. In other cases, this included helping a woman who was convinced she was an angel and being punished by God and exploring why she thought that. In more practical terms the chaplains worked on issues like patients demanding the Halal food option because they thought it looked nicer!

This role in training staff and changing organisational policy was also very much in evidence in Further Education. At one college we visited in a very diverse area, the chaplains were involved in training staff in how to respond and react to students of different faith backgrounds. They had also worked on negotiating a way to hold exams that didn't overly disadvantage those students fasting during Ramadan and were a key part of the college's response to issues like forced marriage, abuse and radicalisation. They advised the college on all those issues and how to run training and design safeguarding policies to reflect that need.

In a number of organisations, including healthcare, further education and higher education a chaplaincy representative often sat on senior committees to give voice to diversity concerns. At one university the chaplain on the student services committee voiced concerns about the way a particular policy would affect Muslim students. At another, the chaplain advised their university over concerns about a controversial speaker to the Islamic society.

This role was more significant in organisations in which the chaplain, as discussed above, was hired at least in part to be an explicitly critical or 'prophetic' figure within the organisation. Chaplains in Christian charities concerned with homelessness were particularly influential in this regard, challenging the organisation anytime it looked like it was losing sight of its purpose or particular calling to help the homeless. Similarly, one sport chaplain had played a role in resisting a payday loan company being chosen as the sponsor for a club and several others had persuaded their clubs to start schemes to tackle gambling abuse among players, or run life skill classes for young players who weren't going to make it at the club.

Other chaplaincies were, on the whole, less concerned with policy or practical changes on the part of the institution. Some simply weren't in a position to have much impact, perhaps because there wasn't such a clear organisation to change or because their role was too peripheral to the management of the organisation. Even in these cases, however, there are examples of some fairly radical changes. One port chaplain for the Apostleship of the Sea had discovered that a large modern ship had no food on board, to the extent that the crew had actually gone on strike, a dramatic gesture in an industry in which seafarers who were seen as complainers were often prevented from finding jobs in the future. Usually the chaplains left a dispute like this to the unions or other services, but on this occasion the chaplain was called to be the broker and played a key role as the advocate for the seafarers, eventually winning the fight on their behalf.

There were chaplaincies in which there was perhaps a disappointment, at least to outsiders, that more change wasn't being created. There were reports of people, religious and otherwise, who hoped that the chaplains of Canary Wharf might be more assertive in criticising the practices of certain banks and bankers, and people who felt that military chaplains might speak up a bit more against particular campaigns, such as the Iraq war, or that a casino chaplain might do more to fight against gambling, rather than support people working in it. Chaplains to Immigration and Removal Centres are likewise religious figures who, at least to outsiders, sometimes seemed insufficiently critical of their own organisation (though they were often very criticial of immigration policy in private). These are difficult issues, and show a tension in the purpose of chaplaincy. While in some contexts chaplains can be advocates and critical figures, in others, were they to perform that role, they would likely cease to be allowed access to those organisations and so would be unable to offer any help to the people in these places. This tension highlights exactly why chaplains and organisations need to be very clear on the mission and purpose of chaplaincy when defining impact.

change in atmosphere and community

This factor of impact is far harder to measure or prove than the one above. A policy either changed or it did not. A practice that has changed because of a chaplain can be shown to have changed. By contrast, creating a change of atmosphere or sense of community is almost invariably a subjective judgement. It is possible to point to the testimony of stakeholders and service users, and these are not without value in this regard, and it is also possible to point to particular examples of success, be that in mediation between groups or a demonstrable change in the relationship between the organisation and other groups.

A good example of the latter is the role of police chaplains. There is some tension in police chaplaincy between a mission to serve primarily or uniquely as a pastoral service for police and a very different role in forming a bridge with community groups.[5] In a number of police services the latter role is a critical component of why police chaplains are appointed, especially in providing links and access to ethnic and faith minority groups that might for whatever reason have a negative perception of the police. One borough commander was very clear on that advantage – "the most important thing [with chaplaincy] has been the inroads into faith communities... it's good for the police reputation". There have been real success stories coming out of this, with lots of examples of police being invited to temples and mosques and increased cooperation between the community and the police.

A homeless charity chaplain had been instrumental in forming links between the charity and local churches, providing a means for raising money for the charity and raising awareness of the work. A prison chaplain was the key broker in forming links between prisoners and churches to form bonds and support networks on their release. This has also been a focus of some community (ex-offender) chaplains. These are all examples of a successful link role between an organisation and the wider community.

Changing the atmosphere and community within an organisation is more difficult to provide evidence for. There are examples of actions taken to confront particular problems that stakeholders at least perceive to have been effective. For example, a university that had been having real problems with tensions between Palestinian and Israeli societies relied heavily on their chaplain to calm those tensions as a trusted broker between both sides. Senior management felt that on the whole this had been a great success. One pointed to a particular example: at the height of an especially difficult period in Israel, the chaplain had been running a Holocaust memorial day and was able to persuade the Palestinian society to make a statement of condolence and solidarity without reference to the current situation in Palestine.

At another university, efforts had been made to try and involve the whole university community in as much as possible, so the carol service included readings from both the Vice-Chancellor and a gardener. This was remembered favourably by a number of students and staff. Little gestures like that can have a lifting effect on a whole organisation. A school chaplain had created a wall of remembrance for students and staff to put up pictures of loved ones who had died. Apart from being moving visually, it had had an important community effect in that staff often discovered a death in a student's family from the wall long before it was fed back to them in some other way. At another school a chaplain had created a programme to work with young girls on issues of confidence and self-esteem. Senior staff were effusive in their praise of this scheme saying that it had created an enormous change in the girls involved and on their friends.

evidence of impact on service users

In the section on pastoral and welfare work above under mission and purpose, an example was drawn from the work of the Apostleship of the Sea in providing very practical help to seafarers in British ports – such as providing access to the internet, local currency, phone cards, etc. This has an enormous impact for seafarers, since cheap means to contact home and get access to funds in different currencies are hard to come by. Interestingly, however, chaplains suspected that that form of provision was probably on its way out – with more and more ships now investing in their own internet and means of communication.

There was a huge number of individual testimonies to the impact of chaplains with service users. For example, chaplains were often asked to perform weddings, baptisms, or funerals, and not only for service users, but for people that they were related to, or were friends with. It is a mark of the esteem in which a chaplain is held that they should be asked to do these services, and not just within their own organisation but for the wider associated circle.

One former service user at a hospital, who now volunteers with the chaplains, reported that "a chaplain literally saved my life". She had been suffering with severe mental distress and had been suicidal before the chaplains had helped her to re-discover a sense of self-worth. Another, at a port, felt so indebted to the chaplain that he invited him to visit his family in India to become a part of the family.

Some of the pastoral work for service users is very direct indeed. For example, in healthcare, hospices and AIDS chaplaincy the chaplain has an immensely important role, in some cases persuading a service user to take their medication. In many of these cases the service user was losing heart to keep on fighting and caring about their treatment – the chaplain was involved in fighting this and making people feel "worthy of being helped" (hospice chaplain). That sense of creating self-worth was also apparent in several other sectors, especially in ex-offender and homelessness chaplaincy. One chaplain noted being asked by a service user, "pray for me please, because I can't". The service user in question was struggling hugely with their self-esteem and any belief in their own worthiness to be saved. Serious illness, imprisonment and homelessness can all have an effect of de-humanising a service user; the chaplain has a powerful potential role in those settings to 're-humanize' a person.

Often overlooked is pastoral work done with secondary service users (i.e. not the primary service users that an organisation expects chaplains to work with). Often there is a perception that chaplains are there for a particular group of people within an organisation, such as patients, prisoners or students. This would be to ignore the amount of work chaplains often do with a wider circle of people. In hospitals this is especially true of working with staff. One paediatric chaplain had been developing a whole programme for work with staff in a children's hospital because so many staff were seeking out the chaplain.

Serious illness, imprisonment and homelessness can all have an effect of de-humanising a service user; the chaplain has a powerful potential role in those settings to 're-humanize' a person.

"There's only so many times you can work with dying children before you start questioning why it happens," he noted. Not that the chaplains were providing glib or easy answers to such questions, but they were helping people explore the questions for themselves. A former senior army officer brought out a similar idea, talking about his experiences in Kosovo.

Evil and sin are not interesting discussions for me – I have seen the mass graves and slaughter. In that environment spirituality is important. It's the moral component of which chaplaincy is a key component.

In other contexts several stakeholders remembered the chaplains helping them during really difficult personal periods. A senior army officer, a shopping centre manager and a university manager were among those who had been helped by a chaplain through a bereavement.

A final impact on service users is the more indirect effect of the advocacy work done by chaplains – such as fighting for Kosher and Halal food, for prayer spaces or for consideration during periods of fasting or religious festivals. This is an often unseen but potentially very significant and important result for organisational service users.

increased support or buy in

Often it is by seeing how organisations have changed the way they relate to their chaplains that provides some of the best evidence for how successful chaplaincy has been. One obvious example of this is when a chaplaincy grows, either within an organisation or perhaps inspiring growth elsewhere.

For example, a police commander was asked by some of his officers to investigate getting a police chaplaincy into their service because they had experienced it elsewhere and wanted to have it available to them again. On the strength of their recommendation he appointed a police chaplain. Town Centre chaplaincy is another of those that has spread gradually in recent years after a good example in one place has inspired growth elsewhere.

One of the best examples, though, has been sport chaplaincy. Sport Chaplaincy UK has always been keen to grow and identify new clubs and sports to find chaplains for, but often this growth is led by the clubs themselves. Certain football managers have gained a reputation for taking chaplains to every new club they go to because they like the service it provides. One rugby club chaplain described how he had originally just been asked to help advise a local club on getting a chaplain and then found himself taken on "almost against my will" by the club!

Even in healthcare some teams have actually seen their funding increase or at least, in other cases, not be cut as much as other non-frontline services. In fact, a BBC FOI request in 2013 revealed that while 40% of NHS trusts had cut the number of chaplaincy hours, 25% had actually increased them since 2009.[6] Good chaplaincies that do important work often grow because their value is obvious to those around them, even if it is sometimes difficult to quantify.

This sense of total organisational support without the ability to identify clearly why that should be was common across a number of fields. A university Vice Chancellor described the new chaplaincy system they've brought in as "the best investment I've ever made". A former deputy Vice Chancellor at another university described their chaplain as "one of the most valued people we've got. What we pay is tiny and what we get is enormous." A police commander admitted that in a time of financial pressure having a chaplain meant potentially having one or two fewer PCSOs "but that's a sacrifice worth making in terms of value to the police".

There was also a sense in a number of interviews of something intangible that would be lost if the chaplain left. A deputy headmistress, for example, talking about the impact of her school's chaplain said:

> A lot of people come into the school and tell you there's something different but they can't tell you what it is. If you could bottle it he would be in that bottle – and we'd miss that a lot if he left.
>
> (Deputy headmistress, Church of England school)

That same sense was mentioned by a former senior army officer:

> If [we] got rid of chaplains we would be the poorer for it – you wouldn't see the results straight away, it wouldn't happen overnight. Over time things would change.

conclusion

Our research revealed a large number of very different stories and accounts of how chaplains have had a profound impact on their organisation. Some of these stories are personal (in that they affect a particular individual) and others are more corporate (an impact upon an organisation as a whole). This section serves to demonstrate the range of these stories and provide examples of how chaplains have accomplished different things in different settings. In the 'pipeline' of chaplaincy impact that began with what chaplaincy is for (its mission and purpose) this section is showing how that aim has been expressed in a practical sense. One thing that these stories do not really demonstrate is why chaplains have been able to be successful. It is to that question that the next section turns.

what enables chaplains to be effective?

So far this part has argued that an analysis of impact demands clarity over what the point of chaplaincy is, what chaplains do and what evidence there is of them being successful. This section takes a step back to look at the factors that have an effect on how impactful a chaplain can be or, in other words, what it is that enables chaplains to be effective. It identifies in particular five issues that are important in this regard:

1.   Religious appeal – the role an explicit religious basis can play in making a chaplain effective;

2.   Personal appeal – the role that an individual by virtue of their personality can have;

3.   Trust and neutrality – many chaplaincies operate with a sort of neutrality from their organisation which is central to their appeal;

4.   Distinctiveness from other services in an organisation;

5.   Facilities and bases – how important are faith spaces and bases for chaplaincy effectiveness?

However, it also recognises that there are factors that inhibit the impact of chaplains. Some of these are noted as points of caution on the five issues above but there are two factors in particular that seem to serve as a particular inhibitor on the impact of some chaplains:

a.   How the structure of a chaplaincy team can serve to help or hinder the effectiveness of chaplaincy;

b.   The issue of qualifications.

The evidence for these themes is again drawn from across the range of interviews. Several of them are open to challenge both from other chaplains and stakeholders and from outsiders, but nonetheless they reflect the evidence we have found. Stakeholder and service user perspectives are of course particularly important here in providing an external vision of why chaplains are important to them and these interviews are prioritised here. The last two notes on inhibiting factors, however, draw more heavily from chaplains themselves on areas that they see as particular difficulties in maximising their role.

religious appeal

Care needs to be taken when talking about religion being an appealing factor in chaplaincy. For one thing not all chaplains are religious. For another, it is possible that for a minority of service users religion is likely to put them off a person more than make them appealing. This is a frequently voiced complaint from the BHA and NSS, both of whom have claimed repeatedly that most (or at least a significant portion of) people do not find chaplains to be appealing precisely because they are religious. The evidence from our interviews on this was mixed. Very few chaplains had ever experienced any hostility towards their role on the basis of being religious. A humanist healthcare chaplain disputed that as a fair finding on the basis that people, in his experience, were often too polite to make a fuss, even if they felt uncomfortable. A Sikh chaplain supported that interpretation because lonely people in a hospital "will talk to anyone – it doesn't mean that person is the best qualified for them to talk to!"

We also heard from a number of stakeholders that they had been a bit unsure about, or even opposed, to chaplains whom they had inherited when they took on their role. A police commander, a member of staff at a court and a manager of a homelessness hostel all admitted in their interviews a sense of discomfort at least at first in the presence of chaplains. This was especially true among stakeholders who were not themselves religious, or when the organisation as a whole had a particularly secular ethos, like some universities.

Those are legitimate concerns, and there were several stakeholders who noted that if there was one criticism they could level at chaplaincy it would be that there is a need to do more to cater to the needs of the non-religious as well as the religious. Many chaplains were already putting considerable effort into doing that, but there is undeniably a difficulty in doing that as a religious person if the service user in question has an issue with religion. It can be a particular point of tension in some organisations where religion might have a poor reputation. Stakeholders and chaplains in theatre chaplaincy conceded that some service users in theatre had particular concerns with organized religion – especially on issues of sexuality. In AIDS chaplaincy the legacy of a historic and present failing of many religious groups to come to terms with or respond to AIDS has also left a difficult legacy for chaplains to confront.

However, there can be no doubt that often it was the religious nature of many chaplains that was central to their appeal to both their organisations and to service users. Being a figure seen to have religious expertise was very important in a number of settings. In dealing with issues over dietary laws and bereavement practices, for example, the religious authority of the chaplain was very important. One healthcare chaplain noted that his expertise on Islamic bereavement work and funerals had made him indispensable to the hospital that was finding things increasingly difficult with Muslim patients. This, of course, is all the more true in the many fields which, as discussed above, rely on their chaplains for advice and consultancy on faith, diversity and inclusion issues.

The authority and expertise in their own faith is especially important in areas like mental health, where chaplains are involved in working with doctors to identify patient beliefs that are the norm for their particular faith, beliefs that are a bit extreme, but still not necessarily dangerous, and patients who exhibit beliefs that are not to do with their faith but may be a part of a wider mental health problem. One Christian chaplain worked with a patient who was convinced she was a demon, and another who thought she was an angel who could fly.

Being able to see, define and explain the limits of a particular faith position is also critical when dealing with issues of extremism and radicalisation. Prisons, universities and colleges are increasingly being expected to monitor and fight Muslim radicalisation. A large proportion of Muslim chaplains are now funded or appointed in part precisely as part of this Prevent agenda. This raises a number of serious problems for the neutrality and appeal of chaplains, as will be discussed below, but it also requires a high level of care and expertise on the part of chaplains. There is a fine line between allowing someone to explore ideas that might degenerate into extreme positions as part of their intellectual development and showing due wariness of the dangers of extremism.

In less extreme circumstances, often the religious appeal of the chaplain is simply in their appropriateness to perform a particular aspect of the role. For example, one hospital recorded that an average of 23 people a week received Holy Communion and there were a great many call outs, particularly for Catholic healthcare chaplains to perform the sacrament of anointing the sick. These are not roles that it is appropriate that any other faith person or non-faith person should perform. If Catholic patients want to be anointed, perhaps because they are about to die, their demands deserve to be met according to their own faith requirements – quite simply no other person, however well-meaning, will do. The same is true of Friday prayers for Muslims, funerals in most religions and a host of other religion-specific activities.

This particularly comes into its own when the issue of rituals comes up. As the section on 'creating community and ethos' above illustrated, rituals can be enormously important to an institution. Some of these are not inherently particularly religious – and yet there is a tradition and appropriateness that seems to mark the chaplain out as especially well-suited. For example, one sports chaplain noted how he and a sports psychologist had a clear understanding that when it came to funerals and bereavement that was the chaplain's area alone unless he needed help. In the military, the traditional role of a chaplain in repatriating dead servicemen and women and performing the funerals is highly regarded.

Furthermore, one interesting finding was the number of chaplains approached by or referred to service users who were no longer members of their former faith community, but still wanted to speak to a chaplain from that group. One Catholic prison chaplain noted how often he was asked to speak to a prisoner whose family might have been Catholic, or who went to Catholic school, but who was no longer Catholic themself. In an environment so utterly divorced from their own family and home, the chaplain was a point of continuity with something from their childhood or past, and had some appeal in that resonance.

There was also some evidence for the appeal of having someone recognisably religious who was prepared to talk about spiritual and religious issues. A theatre chaplain remembered an actor who was convinced there was a religious subtext to a play he was in and wanted to talk about it and explore it, but no one on the production was willing to do so. Statistics from a large mental health NHS Foundation Trust found that only 13% of service users thought spirituality was of no importance to them, and the vast majority of staff thought that spirituality was both important and something that the Trust should address.[7]

personal appeal

It should be little surprise that one of the most important aspects in the appeal of chaplaincy is who the chaplains are. In a role that is often very personal and based on relationships, a non-judgemental attitude and being there for people in need, the personality of a chaplain is a critical element in their impact. In many fields an organisation might have only one chaplain. That makes chaplaincy a particularly difficult role, often requiring enormous energy, self-sufficiency and a high level of confidence in their ability to get alongside people. Even where there is a team of chaplains, it is fair to say that they are not like other roles in an organisation, and as a result the character of a chaplaincy is very reflective of the personalities of the people involved. Accordingly, even within a field there might be very little similarity in the feel and approach of a chaplaincy in one organisation as opposed to another. The range, for example, in how university chaplains describe their role and the way the chaplaincy operates, is enormous.

This does raise a potential problem in terms of sustainability. Some of the chaplains that we encountered had gone so far beyond their required duties and created a ministry so much in their own image that it is difficult to envisage how easy it would be to replicate or replace them. Of course, there is also the danger at the other end of the scale – a bad chaplain can prejudice and destroy the reputation of chaplaincy very quickly, further increasing the need for faith and belief groups in particular to monitor impact and performance.

A theatre company manager gave a good example of this problem. He was, in general, very supportive of theatre chaplains and had only one rule; that chaplains had left the backstage area by 30 minutes before a performance started to let the actors prepare. Several times chaplains had refused to follow that rule and had caused unnecessary friction. Some other company managers were sufficiently annoyed by such behaviour as to not want to work with any theatre chaplain ever again. A police officer also recalled how a chaplain that he had encountered in the past had been "a bit of a bulldozer" and had prejudiced him somewhat against other chaplains until his opinion was changed by a very good chaplain at another police station.

One aspect that came out in a few fields was how advantageous a shared background can be to a chaplain. For example, one sport chaplain to a rugby academy thought that it was a huge advantage he was a former rugby player himself – the young players understood that he really had been through the same struggles. Community chaplains, working with ex-offenders, often involved a number of ex-offenders themselves. The ability to speak the same language (often literally in the case of minority faith or ethnic groups) was an important feature in this. In a number of fields an element of solidarity was important, with police and military chaplains in particular often doing the same training as a means of building relationships and respect.

Not everyone, however, would agree that a common background or interest is necessary or even helpful. The casino chaplain in Luton is there to help staff, but is opposed to gambling. Some sport chaplains were not sporty at all – in fact in one chaplain's case part of his appeal to the club was precisely because he was not a football fan or someone with a background in sport. He was, as a result, absolutely independent of the pressures and tensions affecting other people associated with the club.

All of which is to say that while there is no single 'right answer' to questions of this sort, the personality and background of a chaplain often can be an important aspect in how effective that chaplain is.

trust and neutrality

In almost every field in which we conducted interviews, the theme of the perceived neutrality of the chaplain arose. Often the neutrality is in effect a useful fiction, but one into which everyone seems genuinely to buy.

By way of a few examples – in sport, chaplains were trusted by players far more than other members of the club because they were not really "part of the club". Often, according to several chaplains, players felt too scared to admit personal problems or that they needed time off for fear of being dropped and losing their careers. Chaplains were not seen as part of the club hierarchy and, therefore, were people that could be talked to honestly.

In healthcare a manager and senior nurse both noted the importance of chaplains not being "tainted by diagnosis". Everyone else on the ward tended to have had a role in diagnosis. Only the chaplain was there simply to talk to people, and not necessarily about their condition.

In higher education this theme was summarised by a senior member of a university in the following way:

> He [the chaplain] also has the advantage that he is not of the school. People could speak to him in confidence, they could speak anonymously, they could be angry and say things they regretted. If someone came to me it would almost certainly become an official complaint and I had to deal with it. That layer of confidentiality,

a sort of safety net, was enormously important for me and enormously important for students, they recognise that.

(University Deputy Vice-Chancellor)

In community chaplaincy and in Immigration and Removal Centres, the chaplain's importance lay precisely in not being from the probation service, the immigration service or a lawyer. That differentiation from the authorities and the system was a key enabling factor in the success of chaplaincy. It is also a factor which has been highlighted as a key one in several studies on prisons by Andrew Todd.[8]

This neutrality can be expressed in some very pronounced organisational ways. In the Royal Navy, for example, the chaplain doesn't carry a rank but instead assumes the rank of the person to whom they are speaking – a very clear symbolic statement on their neutrality within an organisational structure. Sports chaplains have traditionally had a very strong stance against being paid by clubs – on the basis that that would undermine their independence and neutrality. Interestingly, though that is important in the way they conceive their role, the evidence from other fields suggests that even paid chaplains are usually able to maintain that aura of neutrality, despite the clear tension with receiving payment directly from an organisation.

What is in common in all these cases is that the role of a chaplain in being able to sit within an organisational setting without being fully part of it is something that was accepted and viewed as a positive by both stakeholders and service users. This should seem surprising. After all, in some fields chaplains are paid and have been part of the provision for decades. Furthermore the public discourse over religion has tended in recent times to assume that religion undermines any sense of neutrality. Secularism, it is often argued, is the only guarantee of neutrality and respect for all faiths and none. Yet when it comes to chaplaincy despite its often clear religious nature and close ties to the organisation, the chaplain is legitimately viewed as an essentially neutral figure by organisations and service users alike, and that neutrality is seen as crucial to the success of their role.

Indeed, while neutrality is increasingly under threat in some sectors the threat seems to be coming more from 'secular' policy than from religious identity. In community chaplaincy there are real concerns that changes in the government's policy on rehabilitation of ex-offenders will effectively eliminate some of the work going on in that area. As one senior figure in a community chaplaincy made clear, their model relies on voluntary work which is independent, albeit cooperating with probation services. Their mentors and chaplains are trusted because of that lack of vested interest and because of a personal relationship. The changes in policy, with much heavier burdens on recording results and payment by results were perceived by some as a threat to the success of that model. It will require the impossible: "caring on an industrial scale".

In other fields, it is being undermined by the battles over Islamic extremism and radicalisation. Already in 2013 there was evidence building of a reaction against Muslim chaplains in prisons as "Home Office imams".[9] This risks the danger, apart from anything else, of policy sawing through the branch on which it sits. If chaplains come not to be trusted by prisoners the chances of them being able to help preventing radicalisation will be reduced. The flip side of this radicalisation debate is that a (contested) report from the Quilliam Foundation alleges that chaplains may be part of the problem when it comes to extremism since they are too often drawn from the conservative Deobandi branch of Islam.[10] If this claim were to be proved (the report itself contained a number of methodological issues and has been widely criticised by chaplaincy groups) that too would fundamentally undermine the neutrality role.

> In the Royal Navy, the chaplain assumes the rank of the person to whom they are speaking – a very clear symbolic statement on their neutrality within an organisational structure.

Similar dangers and fears were expressed in education. The 2006 Promoting Good Campus Relations document issued by the Department for Innovation, Universities and Skills made explicit note of £6 million being available for Muslim chaplaincy to play a role in combatting extremism.[11] One chaplain we interviewed was very worried about the message this would send: "I am not here to spy on students – I am here to help them". Far more caution needs to be used in thinking about how chaplains are being utilised in this fight, or else we risk fundamentally undermining the other missions and purposes discussed above.

distinctiveness from other services within an organisation

This was a factor that arose in many interviews, particularly with service users across different fields. The basic point is that chaplains were effective in large part because they were not like other services available in an organisation. In some cases this was for the very simple reason that there was no other pastoral or welfare service available. A field like waterways chaplaincy, for example, is one in which there are very few pastoral or welfare services available to those who live and work on the canals. However, even in fields with fairly well established and varied welfare provision, like universities, the chaplains retained an appeal in large part thanks to being recognisably different from other services.

One aspect of this is simply being prepared to do things that others aren't prepared to do. One healthcare chaplain described how he had done a funeral for a homeless man. Only one nurse showed up, but it mattered a lot to her. If the chaplain had not been there, he wondered, "Who would bury these people?" A Catholic healthcare chaplain described part of the distinctiveness of his role as being "permanently on call". Where other healthcare professionals went home at the end of their shift, the Catholic chaplain could always be reached in an emergency if the patient requested it. An agricultural chaplain (and many others) echoed that sense of availability: "people know they can call me any time of the day or night and I'll be there".

In fields with a more developed welfare provision, often stakeholders and service users compared what chaplaincy provided to that of other services. For example, at university level counselling was often portrayed as very clinical, oversubscribed, and intimidating for some students who needed some help, but not quite at that level. As one student described her experiences:

> It took me two and a half months to get an appointment with a counsellor. The chaplaincy is there, open, and a lot more approachable in practice. I think students would feel much more comfortable [with chaplains] than going and talking to a proper doctor.
>
> (Student)

Another described it as providing

> mental health help. It's not always as helpful to have the counselling service etc. Once you leave the room, that's it. Sometimes you need a bit less than what they give, but more frequently and more socially.
>
> (Student)

A service user in a totally different setting was similarly critical of their experiences with counselling: "The difference between counsellors and chaplains – counsellors 'try to get into your brain', chaplains *listen*."

Obviously this is a subjective assessment, and universities have put a lot of investment and effort into pastoral and mental health services, as have many other fields in which chaplains operate. The point, however, is not that counsellors do a bad job, but simply that for many service users they prefer a service which is different, and which is often provided by chaplains. The 'softer' and often more informal nature of chaplaincy is often a key aspect in their appeal.

There is also something in the nature of that provision that is appealing in so far as it seems to be more holistic than other services. In healthcare there is something in the work of chaplains that, unlike any other person in healthcare, aims at being "more than a cure".[12] Similar ideas were expressed in a number of sectors along the general idea of chaplains not just trying to "fix" people to the minimum standard but aiming at something more holistic. A company manager for a West End theatre summed this sense up while considering the difference between his pastoral role and that of the chaplain:

Unlike the company manager they're not there to just fix people up enough for the performance. They're all about the individual and the person – actually fixing problems. If you like, she's an actual carer – I'm the GP and she's the surgeon.

(West End Company Manager)

This is also tied into the importance of being known and seen. Where other services might only ever be encountered at a time of emergency, chaplains in many fields have developed a more visible *presence* such that service users know who they are and what they do. This level of familiarity founded on relationships was often described as giving a chaplain an edge over other potential service providers.

This does raise a certain danger to chaplaincies, particularly those that have become very intensely focused on pastoral and welfare work. It is very easy for chaplains to become non-distinctive, and instead just another (often lower paid and lower qualified) part of a wider welfare provision. We did encounter evidence of where this has occurred. An airport chaplain declared that she sometimes felt "like a glorified information clerk". A chaplain to a Council noted that she has to actively force herself to leave her desk because there are so many emails, administrative issues and data recording tasks that if you aren't careful "it gets to the end of the day and you realise you haven't actually helped anyone!". It was also an issue noted in the military. There has been a significant expansion in welfare services in the military over recent years and there was a sense that some chaplains were losing their distinctive identity and being sucked more and more into the same role. Maintaining a distinctive element is vital for a chaplain's impact, or else they might very quickly find themselves made obsolete by the increasing professionalism and spread of other welfare providers.

> *Where other services might only ever be encountered at a time of emergency, chaplains in many fields have developed a more visible presence such that service users know who they are and what they do.*

facilities and bases

In many fields chaplains did not have any sort of base, be that a faith centre, chapel, prayer room, office, or anything else. This was not necessarily problematic. For some, indeed, it was preferable:

I have one colleague who is desperate to have a chaplaincy building. But the longer we don't have one, the happier I am! If you don't have a building there's nowhere to hide, not enough space here so I kick my colleagues out. If we had a building we'd have to do stuff in it and the more we do that, the less we'd get out. We need to get out and grow by speaking to people and saying "will you help us?".

(Workplace chaplain)

However, in other fields, having spaces can be very useful. For Muslim chaplains in particular having a dedicated space for Friday prayers, without constantly battling to book big enough spaces, was a great advantage. For others, having somewhere to take people that was confidential and where they could speak privately without being interrupted or disturbed was important. The importance of chaplaincy space in prisons has been emphasized by Todd and Tipton who found that it provides a "safe space" that can serve as a pressure valve for the whole prison.[13]

In other settings a base is essential to the aim of creating and fostering community. At one university, students praised the fact that the faith centre was a rarity on campus as a space where everything was free, sociable and open. The ability to bring groups together in a single space was often cited as an advantage to creating community cohesion. Increasingly, universities are seeing the advantage of such centres in promoting community cohesion and as a marketing tool for a student service. The LSE's new faith centre is a fascinating example: sitting in a new service centre it has been designed according to the needs of different religious groups, with ablution facilities, prayer space, quiet space, a chapel/ lecture space, public space, and a kitchen area with microwaves and fridges separated according to different dietary requirements. This marks a stark contrast from the previous situation, which had a small Christian space in which no events could effectively be held and, entirely separately, some fairly dingy Muslim prayer spaces. The new space is a world-leading example of a multi-faith facility and a useful tool for the institution in selling itself to an international student body and keeping different groups in a single managed space.

More and more educational establishments are establishing faith spaces of some sort. A 2008 report by the Church of England Board for Education found that 51% of higher education chaplaincies had a chapel, 57% had a prayer or quiet space room, and 65% had a Muslim prayer room.[14] Though there are no data available to prove it, it seems very likely that if repeated today the number with a Muslim prayer room and prayer or quiet space room would both have increased, not least due to the increasing number of Muslim students both from the UK and abroad. A 2013 study found that Catholic societies in particular often valued a physical space – partly because of a higher likelihood than other Christian denominations for the space to serve as a church (providing weekly Mass) and also because Catholics in particular valued the social space of a chaplaincy.[15]

inhibiting factors

While each of the five issues above have particular caveats they are, on the whole, all examples of things that improve the effectiveness of chaplaincy. In the course of our research, we also encountered two issues that seemed to serve as serious potential barriers to the impact of chaplains.

how the structure of a chaplaincy team can serve to help or hinder the effectiveness of chaplaincy

This issue essentially concerns who is appointed to be a chaplain or as part of a chaplaincy team and at what level they are able to be appointed. Any chaplaincy is faced with a decision about how it is managed and who it appoints as chaplains. It is rarely, if ever, practical to represent all religions and faith positions. Nor is it plausible even in large organisations to have a large number of paid full-time chaplains representing different backgrounds and beliefs. How a chaplaincy team deals with this issue is important. In some cases it can lead to some chaplains struggling to have as much impact as they might because of limitations imposed by these questions.

One example of this is the issue of Christian (often specifically Anglican) dominance. A complaint in a number of fields was that there were chaplaincy teams in organisations that were nominally multi-faith but to which, in practice, it was almost impossible to get appointed unless you were from the right faith and belief group. In others the teams were multi-faith, but in practice very few members of the team were paid or full-time, and those that were dominated the team and its management.[16] Anglicans came in for particular criticism from some minority groups who felt excluded by lead chaplains or administrators. A Sikh chaplain claimed to have found it almost impossible to get some NHS chaplaincy teams to have a volunteer Sikh chaplain on their list. Similar complaints were voiced from humanists and pagans among others. Even some Christian chaplains took issue with Anglican colleagues. Some Catholic chaplains in the military and healthcare claimed that Anglican lead chaplains refused to understand the Catholic position about the importance of Catholic sacraments to Catholic patients. A study by Dr Ataullah Siddiqui also argues that Muslim students in Higher Education felt that chaplains from other faiths failed to meet their demands and needs, a finding supported anecdotally by a range of our interviewees.[17]

From the point of view of an organisation, a bias towards Anglicanism has a certain intrinsic sense. As the Established Church, Anglicanism has a clear sense of responsibility for people of all faiths within the UK. It also remains, in terms of census responses, the largest single faith or belief group in the UK. Furthermore, other chaplains were sometimes criticised as being less willing or able to work with service users of different faiths. Catholics were singled out by one senior nurse as being less willing to work with other patients than most other chaplains. Muslim chaplains have been criticised in similar terms for being quite insular, looking after the demands of their own service users but not being willing to engage with people of other faiths.

It is clearly not realistic to expect organisations to pay a full-time chaplain of every faith in the UK – the cost would be enormous and the scale far too large for many organisations that currently want to have chaplains. However, where it becomes a problem is if a team or position is claiming to be 'multi-faith' with the purpose of actively supporting different faiths, but in practice does not do so, marginalising or limiting certain faith groups. It is notable that despite chaplains from other faiths having been a reality in healthcare for some years, there are very few lead chaplains who are not Christians (interestingly this is no longer the case in prison, where Muslim managing chaplains are now if anything over represented and, possibly as a result, there are fewer reported issues over multi-faith relations in chaplaincy teams).[18]

Where minority faith chaplains are limited to lesser roles this can act as a significant barrier to their impact. They might be limited from taking full decisions in the team about the direction of chaplaincy, or from receiving the funding to allow them to expand their role and increase their impact. An unpublished MRes Thesis written in 2014 found that part-time chaplains in a particular healthcare trust were less efficient – they were out of the loop and had limited time to offer to patients.[19]

This was often made worse by the difficulties in hospitals of maintaining a good referral system for different faiths. There were complaints from a number of minority faith chaplains that hospitals were failing to make clear to patients that the option of being referred to a visitor chaplain of their own faith or belief was available to them. In other cases hospitals were simply failing to accurately record a patient's religion, effectively denying them even the option of being referred to a chaplain of their own faith.[20]

There is also a dimension to this in terms of how a chaplaincy team is set up to provide care to their own faith and belief group, or to everyone within an organisation (and, if the latter, is their role a "generic" or inter-faith – effectively faith-blind – role, or is there a religious element ring-fenced?). This matters in terms of enabling a chaplain to do their job because a "generic" model of chaplaincy in which any chaplain sees any service user regardless of their respective faiths has a particular danger in undermining chaplains. It destroys the religious appeal which was discussed above, removes religious-specific actions which are often highly valued, and risks turning chaplains into nothing more than cheap counsellors without a particular identity of their own. Ironically, given the importance noted above of "neutrality", a generic model of chaplaincy that undercuts different religious and belief identities actually undermines trust in chaplaincy. A Catholic healthcare stakeholder had received a number of complaints that Catholic patients had received communion and only later learnt that the chaplain officiating had not been a Catholic. They were extremely upset by this realisation and their distress undermined any benefit that might have derived from that service being provided to them. Honesty, clarity and authenticity as to who a chaplain is and what they believe are important factors in enabling their impact.

qualifications

One issue in particular which contributes to the difficulties of minority faiths in getting appointments as chaplains is an issue of qualifications and assumptions over religious professionalism. In effect, this is the indirect consequence of a type of role that was long dominated by Anglicans. Since most Anglican clergy have both degrees and a high level of pastoral training included in their ordination training, they are fairly highly qualified for the roles they tend to perform as chaplains. Organisation job descriptions and adverts have, accordingly, come to value those markers and put them as job requirements in appointing chaplains.

This is entirely understandable, but does not necessarily translate well into chaplaincy models for other faiths. In many other faiths, there is no equivalent to the pastoral role of an Anglican priest and no pastoral training involved in any religious training. Indeed, as one Sikh chaplain put it "the priests? They don't even usually speak English – it's not what they do". Within Islam there is no single equivalent of a priest role – Imams are prayer leaders, Muftis are preachers, judges and legal scholars, and neither has quite such an explicit pastoral role as is expected of Anglican priests.[21]

Some significant progress is already happening in some areas, with better and more established training programmes and qualifications being developed in many different chaplaincy fields. In Muslim chaplaincy a particular advance has been the role of the Certificate in Muslim Chaplaincy run by the Markfield Institute.

In almost every chaplaincy field the issue of finding qualifications and training that would equip chaplains for their role and be accepted by organisations was mentioned in interviews. A lot of money and effort is being spent by very different chaplaincy bodies and faith and belief groups, yet the difficulty in getting those schemes recognised and ratified was one that arose regularly.

conclusion

In the pipeline of chaplaincy impact that this part has been exploring this section provides evidence of what contexts and criteria best enable or inhibit chaplains' effectiveness. Improving impact is a difficult task, but clarity over the factors that aid or undermine it would help chaplains, faith and belief groups and organisations to have a clearer sense of what might be possible.

part two – references

1   See Ofsted guidance: http://www.ofsted.gov.uk/sites/default/files/documents/surveys-and-good-practice/p/Promoting%20and%20evaluating%20pupils'%20spiritual,%20moral,%20social%20and%20cultural%20development%20(PDF%20format).pdf

2   Gilliat-Ray, Ali, Pattison *Understanding Muslim Chaplaincy* (2013) pp. 108–114.

3   *Ibid* p. 138.

4   BBC News, 'Hospitals set to sack chaplains' 8 August 2006 http://news.bbc.co.uk/1/hi/england/hereford/worcs/5257452.stm Accessed 19 November 2014.

5   An issue well summarised in David Smart's dissertation 'An assessment of how UK police forces have responded in respect of the development of chaplaincy services since the publication of Her Majesty's Inspectorate of Constabulary report 'Diversity Matters' in 2003 and how the value of chaplaincy is now measured within the police service and the community.' (2012)

6   Reported by the BBC "Chaplaincy services cut in 40% of English NHS hospital trusts" 27 June 2013 http://www.bbc.co.uk/news/uk-england-23011620 . Theos research in 2007 (*NHS Chaplaincy Provision in England*, Theos Research paper September 2007) similarly revealed a more complex picture of chaplaincy cuts than is often assumed.

7   Data drawn from Birmingham and Solihull Mental Health NHS Foundation Trust materials.

8   Todd 'Preventing the "Neutral" Chaplain? The Potential Impact of Anti-"Extremism" Policy on Prison Chaplaincy' *Practical Theology*, vol. 6, issue 2, 144–158 (2013) and Tipton and Todd *The Role and Contribution of a Multi-Faith Prison Chaplaincy to the Contemporary Prison Service* (2011).

9   Todd 'Preventing the "Neutral" Chaplain?' (2013).

10 Brandon report for Quilliam Foundation *Unlocking Al-Qaeda: Islamist Extremism in British Prisons* (2009).

11 'Promoting good campus relations, fostering shared values and preventing violent extremism in Universities and Higher Education Colleges' issued by Department for Innovation Universities and Skills p. 11.

12 Hodge 'Chaplains – how are they known?' *Journal of Health Care Chaplaincy* vol. 11 No. 2 Winter (2011) p. 33.

13 Tipton and Todd *Multi-Faith Prison Chaplaincy* (2011).

14 Clines, *Faiths in Higher Education Chaplaincy* (2008) p. 15–16.

15 Guest, Aune, Sharma and Warner, *Christianity and the University Experience: Understanding Student Faith* (2013) pp. 138 –139.

16 This finding is also supported in Swift, *Hospital Chaplaincy in the Twenty-first Century*, 2nd Edition (2014) p. 76.

17 Siddiqui, *Islam at Universities in England: Meeting the Needs and Investing in the Future* (2007).

18   For example, Todd ('Responding to Diversity: chaplaincy in a multi-faith context' in Threlfall-Holmes and Newitt *Being a Chaplain* (2011)) reported that of 425 full-time healthcare chaplains only eight were from faiths other than Christianity (all Muslims).

19   Bryant *Assertion and Assumption: A Single Site Study of Acute Healthcare Chaplaincy* (Unpublished MRes Thesis, University of Birmingham 2014) p. 38–39.

20   *Ibid.*

21   Gilliat-Ray, Ali, Pattison *Understanding Muslim Chaplaincy* (2013) p. 26.

evaluating, presenting and increasing impact

Based on the findings in the previous part, this part offers a model for chaplains and organisations to better present and increase their impact in the future. For all parties involved in chaplaincy, this process is of critical importance.

For chaplains themselves, a frequent complaint has been that they feel isolated and lacking in support from either the organisation, their faith or belief group or both. A better system for informing people about their work and how things are going would help fill that need. For the organisation in which the chaplain sits, having a more robust impact assessment can help them evaluate how things are going, how resources are being used and how they can better support a valuable service. For a faith and belief group, chaplains present a huge opportunity for engagement in the public square, and a significant potential asset, but one that often seems tangential to the central mission of these groups. A better appreciation of impact might awaken a greater interest in this ministry and highlight to faith and belief groups what chaplaincy can provide – as well as allowing them to check what chaplains are doing in their name.

It is also simply a matter of doing due diligence. There are wonderful stories of what chaplains are doing, but it would be naïve and dangerous to assume that, therefore, there is no need for proper assessment and accountability. The stakes for chaplaincy are potentially quite high – success serves as a powerful ministry that can deliver huge benefits to service users and make a strong case for the position of faith and belief groups in the public square. If done badly, however, chaplaincy as a whole could suffer a loss of reputation and deprive both those who rely on the services, organisations as a whole and the faith and belief groups from which chaplains come, from receiving any of these benefits. It is not sustainable to fail to collect evidence of impact, or to assume that a lack of accountability, however desirable that freedom may seem, does not pose a threat to the chaplaincy model.

The issue is how actually to do this assessment in a way that does justice to the complexity of the impact question brought out in the previous part. To that end what is proposed is a pipeline of assessment that can be adapted to the particular organisational setting in which the chaplain finds himself or herself:

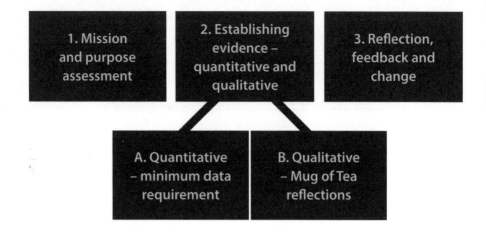

1. mission and purpose assessment

From the previous part it should be clear that a crucial and often overlooked part of this process is real clarity on the part of organisations and chaplains over what exactly is expected of them. Many chaplaincies do have mission statements or job descriptions, but many of these need to be revisited in light of the various purposes of chaplaincy highlighted in the previous part. A full, frank description of what organisations want from their chaplains must be a priority: unless this is clear there is no real way of evaluating how successful chaplaincy is in its particular context. There is no way of knowing what to measure unless the criteria are agreed upon.

Some chaplaincy fields are better at this than others. Further Education has developed a set of seven different benchmarks by which to assess chaplains, each rated either inadequate, satisfactory, good or outstanding.[1] These benchmarks are: Faith, belief and values within the college; Teaching and learning; Pastoral care and spiritual support; Community cohesion and partnerships; Building a multi-faith team; Religious customs; and Student groups. If more fields could emulate this series of benchmarks and establish exactly what is expected of chaplaincy then it will be easier for both chaplains and organisations to develop assessment means that suit those requirements.

2. establishing evidence

Once the mission and purpose are clear it is possible to start building the evidence base. This, realistically, must consist of two parts. First, there is a need for good, hard data. On the one hand, data often become meaningless in these analyses. How can one possibly systematically record some of the activities chaplains engage in? A meeting that is just a catch-up chat might be of huge importance to the service user, or it might not be. If recording meetings, how does one differentiate in raw data between a suicide intervention and simply popping in for a cup of tea? Obviously, this is a huge limitation and necessitates a proper qualitative evaluation of some of a chaplain's work.

Equally data can be very useful if used correctly – at least as a minimum requirement. For example, if a chaplaincy team were to collect data for visits and conversations they had had on a monthly basis and one chaplain had visited significantly fewer service users than their colleagues it would be a fair question to ask how much impact such an individual can realistically be expected to have had. What have they actually been doing with their time? In some cases indeed, data can be illustrative of the extraordinary range of work chaplains are doing.

Accordingly, this evidence must contain both Quantitative (A) and Qualitative (B) elements.

A. quantitative – what data to gather

Which data to collect as a minimum basis for assessment will naturally vary from field to field and organisation to organisation. Even within an organisation it might vary from chaplain to chaplain according to whether they are full-time or part-time.

What the data are designed to show will also vary. For example, data can be used to show a minimal level of activity for different chaplains. An unpaid part-time fire service chaplain, for example, recorded that between 1st April and 31st June 2014 alone she put in 168 hours of work and 1,887 miles of driving to chaplaincy work, including two funerals, bereavement support, a baptism, policy and procedure meetings, and 44 separate visits to fire stations across the county. Collecting data of this sort is good for establishing the range and frequency of activities and demonstrating to organisations a base level of activity.

Some organisations have built up quite sophisticated models for tracking activity. The Chaplaincy Electronic Encounter Record System (CHEERS) used by some NHS trusts, for example, records pastoral care, prayer, anointing, sanctuary services, communions, funerals, teaching, bereavement services, staff support, marriages, carer support, prayers of commendation, and sacraments of the sick, along with how many times each patient has been visited and whether any of those were out of hours.

Some chaplains had developed their own bespoke models. One homelessness chaplain, for example, kept personal records on his different encounters, the sort of work done, and why it had mattered in each case. A sport chaplain had similarly developed his own way of recording what he had been doing and areas to prioritise in the future.

Another form of data that can be valuable is that which demonstrates not only activity but demand. The danger of only measuring activity is that a chaplain might go and see a lot of people, but not actually be needed by them. By contrast, data that measure demand can better demonstrate an organisation's need for chaplaincy. One annual report from a hospital recorded 201 emergency call outs for chaplains, including call outs for out-of-hours advice on 52 occasions. In total, they had 827 referrals across the year and made over 14,600 visits. An average of 23 patients each week received Holy Communion within this one hospital.

Activity and demand between them probably constitute the most basic minimum data requirement for chaplaincies. However, depending on the field there can be some powerful additional data that can be helpful in sketching out the impact of chaplaincy. Two fields in particular that come to mind are those of community chaplaincy (working with ex-offenders) and healthcare chaplaincy.

Community chaplaincy is a field that lends itself to the collection of data on re-offending rates and recidivism. Chaplaincy bodies record a lot of performance indicators including the perception of clients on how their work on drugs, relationships, finding housing, and other factors helps their re-entry into the community.

Different projects (and there are some 25 across the UK) cumulatively reach some 1,400 prisoners and ex-offenders and some of those can also point to some significant claims on figures like re-offending. For example, one project that was involved in our research claims that their clients collectively, compared to ex-offenders not in their programme, show a 40% reduction in the number of offences in the year after prison than in the year before. Others are able to provide data that demonstrate how the severity and frequency of offences is reduced. This is also supported by research from Canada where one study of 60 high-risk offenders found significantly lower levels of recidivism among the participants in a particular community chaplaincy body than among those who did not participate. This included 70% less recidivism in sexual crimes, 57% less recidivism in violent crime, and 35% less recidivism of any kind. Another study found 83% less sexual recidivism, 73% less violent recidivism, and 71% less of any kind overall.[2]

Some of these data are open to challenge and are often drawn from a small sample – which again is illustrative of the need to combine this data approach with qualitative work – but nonetheless these figures are impressive and worthy of being measured *as part of* the impact assessment. Community chaplaincy is unusual in having an objective, as the name suggests, of supporting communities as well as the ex-offenders – so a minimum data requirement that looks at the community impact in these terms makes sense in context.

Healthcare is another area that lends itself to quantification. There have been efforts, having some success in recent years, to draw correlations between positive spirituality and swifter medical recovery.[3] In chaplaincy terms, apart from recording a significant amount of data about what chaplains actually do, healthcare chaplains are sometimes able to record a demonstrable impact on patient wellbeing.

Research by Kevern and Hill has looked at a representative sample of service users of primary care in Sandwell, West Midlands, which uses WEMWBS (Warwick and Edinburgh Mental Wellbeing Scale).[4] Using before and after data from that scale they have been able to demonstrate a notable improvement in wellbeing among those service users who used the Primary Care Chaplaincy service, which also indicated that those most in need received the most help. They also suggest that frequent attenders of GP services become less frequent after seeing chaplains, actually saving money on GP consultancy. Not all NHS trusts use this scale, but those that do could benefit from repeating that study with other chaplains as a mark of the impact of chaplaincy.

Such data are not necessarily useful in all contexts. The point of this section is simply to propose that more innovative data sets could be generated to measure and assess work done towards a particular mission and purpose. Such data can never be the whole story, but they would serve as a useful minimum measure of what is going on in a particular chaplaincy context. There is always a danger (and it was mentioned in a few interviews, particularly in healthcare) of spending too much time recording and tracking data at the expense of core chaplaincy work. That is a real threat and something which has to be managed carefully. Nevertheless, collecting a minimum data set is now an unavoidable part of what most chaplaincies are going to be expected to do. Better databases or recording systems might significantly ease the time burdens on collecting data and are something that faith and belief groups might in particular consider investigating further.

B. qualitative – what to collect and how

The danger with stressing the need for qualitative assessment alongside quantitative is the risk of failing to record anything of real use. To be a fair and critical process, qualitative assessment must rely on more than sporadic anecdotal evidence from chaplains, and should be able to speak to particular criteria. Several different efforts have been made at doing this in different settings but the two that seem most useful are the Values Based Reflective Practice (VBRP) method employed in Scottish healthcare and the Mug of Tea (MoT) method being used in the Methodist Church.

VBRP is "a remarkable vision for mutual learning among healthcare professionals and chaplains through Values Based Reflection groups."[5] It has received funding from the Scottish government as part of a wider desire to help, support and improve staffing in Scottish healthcare. Essentially it involves training groups in reflective practice. They are trained to respond to stories in three different ways – noticing, wondering and realizing. They engage with a number of questions including "whose need was being met and how?" and "what does it tell me about my pastoral ability?" The process ends with participants sharing how their reflection will inform their future practice.

In his report, Ewan Kelly, Director of NHS Education for Scotland's Healthcare Chaplaincy and Spiritual Care programme, suggests that this process has been very successful. It received excellent feedback and 83% of those chaplains surveyed on their experiences felt that their resilience had been enhanced, with many feeling a new sense of fulfilment in their work. There are hopes to roll out the process further in order to build up and encourage other practitioners within Scottish healthcare.

Impressive as that undoubtedly is, this approach does not quite do what is needed in terms of determining and improving impact. It is too focused on the personal development and practice of the chaplains (as opposed to the organisational objectives) and is saturated with Christian terminology that may translate poorly into other fields. All of which is not to say that VBRP is not a potentially very valuable tool for chaplains – simply that it may not provide the organisational impact assessment necessary across the wider range of chaplaincy activity.

For that, a better model might be the Mug of Tea (MoT) approach that has been developed by the Methodist led "Chaplaincy Everywhere" project and the University of Bristol.[6] MoT requires a collector to gather short stories (told in the length of time it takes to have a cup of tea) from different people within an organisation on something that chaplaincy has been involved in. To be most effective it requires a neutral approach that gathers both negative and positive stories.

These stories are recorded and transcribed, then explored by 'reflectors', who are one step removed from the chaplaincy itself (e.g. managers or other people within the organisation). In particular, there is a focus on detecting the Most Significant Change (MSC) that comes out from each story. These stories and reflections are then shared at meetings in which themes and learning are drawn out and discussed between chaplains and stakeholders. [7]

The advantage of this approach versus VBRP is that while it allows for the same types of reflection and personal growth, it also creates an opportunity for organisational objectives and practices to be involved. Part of the intention is to enhance accountability, transparency, participation, and collaboration between the chaplains and organisational structures. This should be of direct benefit to all parties involved. In the case of some chaplaincies it might well be appropriate to include faith and belief group stakeholders in the same or parallel process so that they too can reflect and manage their mission and purpose and assess the impact of their chaplains. At the very least, faith and belief groups ought to adapt something similar even if parallel to or outside the organisation as part of their efforts to engage with, support and resource chaplaincy as a major asset.

The use of this qualitative technique should also help to engage better with some of the issues raised in section 2 above. Often there is a focus within organisations on collecting evidence but in a way that fails to focus sufficiently on the mission and purpose of the various parties involved as criteria for impact. By calling on stakeholders to reflect with chaplains there should be a stronger pull to explore both different missions and purposes and also what factors within the control of those involved can be changed when it comes to enablers and inhibitors.

3. reflection, feedback and change

The section above has already hinted at how change can be brought about to improve chaplaincy and help address issues raised in part 2. The important aspect of this is to see how both the quantitative and qualitative aspects need to be reflected on as organisations, faith and belief groups and chaplains themselves come to think about their work, why it matters and how to improve it in the future. It goes without saying that such a process is one that needs to be done often to keep everyone in the loop about where things are going, flagging up problems and demonstrating the positives that chaplains can bring to their setting.

Using the pipeline proposed above it is hoped that more and more chaplaincies might be able to adopt better means of recording, presenting and improving their impact. As an example of how such a process might work the diagram below shows how a particular organisational mission and purpose might be expressed through the pipeline:

Field: Police chaplaincy

1. Mission and purpose assessment	2. Establishing evidence – quantitative and qualitative	3. Reflection, feedback and change
To provide a link between the police and local community groups	quantitative and qualitative	Police to increase visits to group to strengthen bond. Chaplain needs more volunteers to help reach other groups

A. Quantitative – minimum data requirement	B. Qualitative – Mug of Tea reflections
Records kept of meetings between chaplain and local groups and number of visits of senior police to new community centres	Stories recorded of visits to local groups and what came out of them. Stories of perceptions of change in relationships.

The example above is nothing more than a very brief visualisation of a single aspect of impact on a particular organisational mission. It may well be that for some missions and purposes no change is required, but the reflection maintains its value in proving to the organisation that its resources are being well used and giving both stakeholders and chaplains a chance to make their case for what might change in the future.

conclusion

This part has been focused on learning the lessons from part 2 and proposing new ways to present and build upon the impact of chaplaincy in certain settings. It has been kept necessarily broad for the simple reason that, as part 1 showed, the breadth of chaplaincy is so enormous as to defy much specificity. Nonetheless, it is hoped that the pipeline proposed should have validity and utility across chaplaincy. A lot of immensely valuable work is done in chaplaincy which is very often unseen or difficult to quantify for organisations that are under pressure to demonstrate the impact of every aspect of their organisation. Accountability and impact can no longer afford to be theoretical ideas for many chaplaincies; they are necessities.

There is more to this than being simply defensive, however. Chaplaincy is a powerful potential resource for both organisations and faith and belief groups in meeting a wide range of missions and purposes. This pipeline is designed not to be negative (fending off attacks) but to be positive – looking for ways to improve upon and optimise a ministry that already contains a vast amount of impressive work. For faith and belief groups in particular, given the value of chaplaincy to them in the modern public square there needs to be a greater priority given to strengthening and improving the impact of their chaplains.

part 3 – references

1   Guidance document of the Learning and Skills Council (LSC) and the National Council of Faiths and Beliefs in Further Education (FBFE) *Multi-faith Chaplaincy: A Guide for Colleges on Developing Multi-faith Student Support* (2007), pp. 25–26.

2   Kelly Richards and Philip Whitehead, 'The Journey of the Role of Religious Faith in Corrections: the case of Circles of Support and Accountability' in *International Journal of Community Chaplaincy* (2013).

3   Notably Koenig, McCullough and Larson *Handbook of Religion and Health* (2001) pp. 52–97

4   Kevern and Hill *'Chaplains for Wellbeing' in Primary Care: results of a retrospective study*. Primary Healthcare Research and Development (2014).

5   Kelly, E. 'Translating Theological Reflective Practice into Values-Based Reflection: A Report from Scotland'. *Reflective Practice: Formation and Supervision in Ministry* 33 (2013).

6   http://www.opensourcechaplaincy.org.uk/chaplaincy-everywhere/ Accessed 4 December 2014.

7   The 'Mug of Tea Stories Pack' is available to download at http://www.opensourcechaplaincy.org.uk/wp-content/uploads/2013/07/Mug-of-tea-stories-pack-March-2014with-annexes.pdf Accessed 4 December 2014.

conclusion

the future of chaplaincy and chaplaincy as the future

challenges for the future

Parts 1 and 2 of this report drew respectively on quantitative and qualitative research Theos conducted into chaplaincy. Neither of these sections offered any recommendations or policies in relation to that evidence. Part 3 suggested, based on the qualitative research in particular, that a better model of impact assessment is essential for chaplaincy. However, there are a number of other themes that were important findings from the research which merit inclusion here as a challenge that either chaplains, faith and belief groups, organisations, or some combination of those will have to address.

1. Recording and acknowledging

This research has highlighted the scale of chaplaincy and also the extent to which chaplaincy is dominated by unpaid volunteers who are not themselves religious professionals (e.g. priests, imams etc.). It has also suggested that many faith and belief groups simply do not know about many of the chaplains their faith is providing to organisations. If we accept that chaplaincy provides an important potential asset to faith and belief groups in the UK, then tracking and acknowledging these chaplains ought to be a priority for such groups, otherwise it will be extremely difficult ever to maximize the potential impact of these chaplains. This will require a serious effort at investigating chaplaincy in all the different fields to establish the extent of chaplaincy for each faith and belief group.

2. Funding

Part 1 demonstrated that chaplaincy only rarely receives significant public (or indeed any) funding. Indeed, a high proportion of chaplains themselves are either entirely unpaid or receive only expenses or honoraria. Nonetheless, funding is important in meeting various costs, notably the cost of training. This raises a question of faith and belief bodies in particular. Given the advantages chaplaincy can provide them with, decisions have to be taken about how they can provide that funding most productively to maximise impact. The question becomes one of priorities: are faith and belief groups prepared to absorb the costs of chaplaincy in order to reap the potential benefits or do they wish to prioritise spending elsewhere? Equally for organisations benefiting from chaplaincy perhaps questions should be asked as to whether the benefit they receive from chaplaincy could not be improved further by contributing towards those costs, particularly if they are hoping for more chaplaincy hours.

3.   Volunteers and training

Chaplains are changing the picture of what religious engagement in the public square looks like. This research has shown that chaplaincy is no longer dominated by paid Christian clergy but is now a predominantly voluntary role taken on by those who are not typical religious professionals. This raises both an interesting opportunity and a real challenge to faith and belief groups. On the one hand, chaplaincy provides a resource and expression for a serious and powerful vocation for those who have not typically been involved in ministry. Yet with that comes the need for developed, accredited and useful training to properly equip those people acting in the name of a particular faith or belief group. Many different types of chaplaincy training already exist of course, but the onus must be on faith and belief groups to ensure that more is done to support and train a vital vocation, particularly for those volunteers who are not typical religious professionals.

4.   The future of multi-faith

Many chaplaincy teams are at the forefront of working out issues of how different faith and belief groups interact together towards a common purpose in the public square. This can be a constructive and positive process but it also raises serious questions. When minority faith and belief groups complain about not getting a fair hearing, particularly for management roles in chaplaincy, it can be a real problem. More generally, there is an issue with organisations and institutions that often see chaplaincy in terms of the Christian (most commonly Anglican) model of priesthood and pastoral care. As a result, job descriptions particularly for senior posts often seem to prioritise that model, with preference going to ordained ministers with higher education degrees and a strong pastoral basis to their religious training. This does not fit well into the religious traditions of other faiths and belief groups and it is an issue that organisations and faith groups must both wrestle with in terms of considering how to understand the desire to have multi-faith chaplaincy and what that actually means in practice for different groups. Minority faith groups in particular need to be thinking about what chaplaincy means in a non-Christian context and whether the ideal model is to reflect traditional Christian approaches or to tread a new path.

conclusion

This report began with two stories. On the one hand, there is a story of the decline of UK religion and the triumphant, inevitable march of secularism. On the other, there is the story of chaplaincy, a phenomenon that is spreading further and further across British institutions and organisations. What does this paradoxical relationship mean for both religion and for organisations in British society?

Chaplaincy is not a new form of ministry (at least in Christianity; it is, obviously, more novel in other religious and non-religious traditions). Recognisable chaplains and similar ancestor ministries go back at least into the 19th century, and not only in the "traditional" chaplaincy fields like the military, hospitals and prisons. There was a police chaplain in London in the 19th century and industrial chaplaincy too can trace its roots back into early industrialisation.[1] The Actors' Church Union, with figures not unlike chaplains, began in 1898.[2] The Apostleship of the Sea began work in 1922. These examples notwithstanding, chaplaincy is a ministry that has been growing and even taking centre stage in the way faith and belief groups operate in society.

There is clearly something appealing about the way in which chaplaincy suits and supports organisations in society even as attendance of religious services declines. It represents, in fact, a very modern ministry. It is a ministry that is innovative, fitting in with the way British

Chaplaincy fits especially well into modern British society.

society is, rather than how religious and belief groups might hope it to be; a ministry that provides real practical benefits (as part 2 has illustrated) and services for organisations on their terms, as well as for religious groups alone; a ministry that goes to where people actually are, rather than waiting for them to come to religion. As a result chaplaincy fits especially well into modern British society.

This process, by which chaplaincy is becoming a key constituent part of the public face of faith and belief groups, is already underway whether faith and belief groups recognise it or not. The findings from part 1 suggest not only that chaplaincy is spread throughout British locations and organisations but that the way it is being done does not reflect the traditional model of how religious groups operate. The process is increasingly reliant upon the ministry of lay people, with or without the training and knowledge of their own faith and belief group, and is also reliant upon voluntary efforts. The era of the single paid chaplain sitting within an institution is already over in many fields and is coming to an end in many others. Faith and belief groups can either act to resource, support and embrace this movement or they can let it continue organically and run the risk of losing any control they might have over a powerful resource.

However, this spread and future also requires a more nuanced and dedicated approach to the question of impact. In order to maximise the effectiveness of chaplains, both from the point of view of organisations appointing chaplains and their faith and belief groups, a new system of presenting, evaluating and improving impact is needed. This report has suggested one possible way of doing this in part 3.

The future of chaplaincy needs careful consideration. The well-publicised cuts to some healthcare chaplaincies show how fragile their position can be, and better analysis of impact will be a key part of that conversation in the future. However, it is also an exciting future. Chaplains are everywhere, and their role is growing. Their impact not only on organisations but on their own faith and belief group is often overlooked and is worthy of considerably greater attention.

conclusion – references

1   See, for example, Torry (2010) *Bridgebuilders: Workplace Chaplaincy – A History.*

2   Hole (1934) *The Church and the Stage: The Early History of the Actors' Church Union.*

bibliography

Armitage, Richard Norris, 'Issues of religious diversity affecting visible minority ethnic police personnel in the work place' Ph.D. thesis, (University of Birmingham, 2007).

Bickley, Paul *The State of Play* (Bible Society 2014).

Brandon, James, *Unlocking Al-Qaeda: Islamist Extremism in British Prisons* (Quilliam Foundation, 2009).

Bryant, Joanna *Assertion and Assumption: A Single Site Study of Acute Healthcare Chaplaincy* (Unpublished MRes Thesis, University of Birmingham, 2014).

Camp, Michael and Neave, Garry '"The Public Face of God": Chaplaincy in Anglican Secondary Schools and Academies in England and Wales'. (Church of England Archbishops' Council Education Division and The National Society 2014).

Catholic Bishops' Conference of England and Wales Department for Christian Responsibility and Citizenship Healthcare Reference Group, 'Caring for the Catholic Patient: A Guide to Catholic Chaplaincy for NHS managers and Trusts' (Catholic Truth Society, 2007).

Clines, Jeremy *Faiths in Higher Education Chaplaincy* (Church of England Board of Education, 2008).

Gilliat-Ray, Sophie, Ali, Mansur and Pattison, Stephen *Understanding Muslim Chaplaincy*, (Ashgate, 2013).

Grüneberg, Ian *Report for the National Association of Chaplains to the Police* (2013).

Guest, Mathew, Aune, Kristin, Sharma, Sonya and Warner, Rob *Christianity and the University Experience: Understanding Student Faith* (Bloomsbury, 2013).

Hancocks, G., Sherbourne, J. and Swift, C. "'Are they Refugees?' Why Church of England Male Clergy Enter Health Care Chaplaincy." *Practical Theology* 1: 163–179 (2008).

Heskins, Jeffrey and Baker, Matt *Footballing Lives: As Seen by Chaplains in the Beautiful Game* (Norwich: Canterbury Press, 2006).

Hodge, Debbie 'Chaplains – how are they known' *Journal of Health Care Chaplaincy* vol. 11 No. 2 Winter (2011).

Hole, D *The Church and the Stage: The Early History of the Actors' Church Union* (Faith Press, 1934).

Isaac, Les and Davies, Rosalind *Faith on the Streets* (Hodder and Stoughton, 2014).

Kelly, E. 'Translating Theological Reflective Practice into Values Based Reflection: A Report from Scotland'. *Reflective Practice: Formation and Supervision in Ministry* 33 (2013).

Kevern, P and Hill, L *'Chaplains for Wellbeing' in Primary Care: results of a retrospective study. Primary Healthcare Research and Development* (2014).

Koenig, Harold, McCullough, Michael and Larson, David *Handbook of Religion and Health* (OUP, 2001).

Kotze, Justin 'Developing Collaborative and Sustainable Networks of Social Support: Community Chaplaincy, Faith Communities and the Successful Reintegration of Ex-Prisoners' *International Journal of Community Chaplaincy* (2013) Issue 1.

Learning and Skills Council (LSC) and the National Council of Faiths and Beliefs in Further Education (FBFE) *Multi-faith Chaplaincy: A Guide for Colleges on Developing Multi-faith Student Support* (2007).

Legood, Giles *Chaplaincy: The Church's Sector Ministries* (Cassel Company, 1999).

Marchetto, Agostino 'Pastoral Care of Human Mobility in The Universities of Europe' (Pontifical Council for the Pastoral Care of Migrants and Itinerant People 2004).

Mowat, Harriet 'The Potential for Efficacy of Healthcare Chaplaincy and Spiritual Care Provision in the NHS (UK),: A Scoping Review of Recent Research (NHS, 2008).

O'Hanlon, Andrew *A Brief Guide to Quaker Chaplaincy* (Quaker Life, 2014).

Pattison, Stephen, 'Religion, Spirituality and Healthcare: Confusions, Tensions, Opportunities.' *Health Care Analysis*, 3: 189–92. (2013).

Richards, Kelly and Whitehead, Philip 'The Journey of the Role of Religious Faith in Corrections: the case of Circles of Support and Accountability' in *International Journal of Community Chaplaincy* (2013) Issue 1.

Siddiqui, Ataullah *Islam at Universities in England: Meeting the Needs and Investing in the Future* (2007).

Spencer, Nick and Ritchie, Angus *The Case for Christian Humanism* (Theos, 2014).

Smart, David, Dissertation 'An assessment of how UK police forces have responded in respect of the development of chaplaincy services since the publication of Her Majesty's Inspectorate of Constabulary report 'Diversity Matters' in 2003 and how the value of chaplaincy is now measured within the police service and the community.' (2012)

Sullivan, Winnifred Fallers *A Ministry of Presence: Chaplaincy, Spiritual Care and the Law* (University of Chicago Press, 2014).

Swift, Christopher *Hospital Chaplaincy in the Twenty-first Century*, 2nd Edition (Ashgate, 2014).

Swinton, J. "A Question of Identity: What does it mean for healthcare chaplains to become healthcare professionals?" *Scottish Journal of Healthcare Chaplaincy*, 6(2), pp. 2–8. (2013).

Theos Research Paper, *NHS Chaplaincy Provision in England* (Theos 2007).

Threlfall-Holmes, Miranda and Newitt, Mark *Being a Chaplain* (SPCK, 2011).

Tipton, Lee and Todd, Andrew *The Role and Contribution of a Multi-Faith Prison Chaplaincy to the Contemporary Prison Service* (2011).

Todd, Andrew, Slater, Victoria and Dunlop, Sarah *The Church of England's Involvement in Chaplaincy* Research Report for The Mission and Public Affairs Council (2014).

Todd, Andrew 'Preventing the "Neutral" Chaplain? The Potential Impact of Anti-"Extremism" Policy on Prison Chaplaincy' *Practical Theology*, vol. 6, issue 2, 144–158 (2013).

Todd, Andrew *Military Chaplaincy in Contention: Chaplains, Churches and the Morality of Conflict* (Ashgate, 2013).

Torry, Malcolm *Bridgebuilders: Workplace Chaplaincy – A History* (Canterbury Press, 2010).